# 마이 코리아
# Bearing My Seoul

## Welcome to 1/3 of the
*Bearing My Seoul* experience

### Thanks for getting a print copy of the book.
While there's nothing like the feeling of holding a book and flipping through each page, there's also nothing like hearing an author read you their own story in their own voice with a soundscape that transports you onto location.

### You definitely want the audio experience.
Also, you'll notice as you read along that a big part of the experience is links in the footnotes. There are all sorts of goodies from music videos to news articles.

### Links are only available in the ebook.
Through the ebook, you'll get every drop of backstory from the footnotes with easy access to every film, song, and news story mentioned in the book. You know you want it!

### Get whatever part you're missing at
*bearingmyseoul.com*

# 마이 코리아
# Bearing My Seoul

## Tales of a black American girl in a big Asian city

## Taryn Blake

Gold
Apple
Books

*While the essays in this book are retellings of the author's factual experiences, some names have been changed to afford those mentioned their privacy.*

GOLD APPLE BOOKS

*Bearing My Seoul*
Copyright © 2021 Taryn L. Blake

All internet links were accurate at the time of printing. If you discover an error, please let us know at *hello@goldapplebooks.com*.

Library of Congress Control Number: 2021914631

First Edition: November 2021
Printed in the United States of America

ISBN:   978-17379784-04 (paperback)
        978-17379784-35 (hardcover)
        978-17379784-11 (audiobook)
        978-17379784-28 (ebook)

Korea: Thanks for the memories.
Let's make more soon.

# Contents

안녕 하세 요!

# The Intro

Hi friends!

Seoul, Korea, is one of the largest metropolitan areas on the planet. It consistently ranks among the Top 10. That comes with Top 10 noise, pollution, busy sidewalks, crowded trains, and teeny, tiny apartments.

Seoul is also *lit.er.al.ly* "The City that Never Sleeps." Bars and clubs stay open as long as they have patrons (typically about 5:30 a.m. when the trains start up again). If one place closes, there's always another place within walking distance. If not a bar, a café. If not a café, then karaoke. If not karaoke, pull up a plastic chair outside the neighborhood convenience store and crack open a soju 'cuz that's how Seoul gets down.

Any place that is so perpetually busy is bound to have elements of chaos—that's the "bearing" portion of *My Seoul* in the book's title. But like residents of other iconic cities, I was in no rush to leave.

I love Seoul like New Yorkers love New York City. If you've never met any New Yorkers, let me sum up that NYC type of love:

NEW YORKER
(to No One in Particular)
"Why do I live in this dirty, overcrowded city, paying $2,000 a month for a shoebox?"

RANDOM PASSERBY
Because there's no place like it on earth!

NEW YORKER
(to Self)
He's right! Those bums in Colorado can keep all that fresh air.

Yup. That kinda love.

My one-year teaching contract turned into over five years in Seoul from August 2008 to March 2014.

For those of you who don't know me—which is half the people reading this book—I'm American of the "regular black" variety. It's also worth noting that

I'm Christian[1] which informs—amongst a myriad of other things—my obsession with Biblical parallels for random circumstances as well as my decision to go on a date with a particular Korean deportee and misguided emulator of hip-hop culture against my better judgement. (See: "Thug Life.")

I lived in the Seoul suburbs—방화, 가양, 부천—and in 이태원 downtown. I rode public transportation and I eventually bought a car. I met lots of people and I did lots of stuff. That's what the stories in this book are about.

Speaking of which: Thank you for buying my book! I'm so geeked that you're reading this. This book isn't fiction. I've been telling these stories in one way or another since they happened. I wrote each essay to match what happened as closely as I remember it. They've been sitting on my laptop for quite some time begging me to put them out into the world. (*Yay. I did it!*)

And on a final personal note, while this may be obvious to most, it's worth mentioning that memoir is a recording of particular moments in time. The reactions and conclusions I've written here are just that—*written*. People and places are not fixed. They are always pulsating with change and hopefully, progress for the better. (Myself included!)

---

[1] And by "Christian" I mean that I follow the teachings of Jesus to the best of my ability. I'm getting better at it every day!

One of the most distinctive things about Korea is how lightening fast the country changes. Modern Korea is just barely "over the hill." It hasn't yet settled into the steady rhythms of old age. It's still fighting over, and for, its legacy. Fighting like hell. Literally. (Do an internet search for "South Korean National Assembly fights" for reference.[2]) But hey, let's hear it for democracy, their neighbors to the North are nearly as lucky.

Seoul will forever live on in my heart—and by the publishing of this book—on these pages. With that in mind, I welcome you to experience snapshots of a whirlwind season of my life in a whirlwind metro of a city.

Thank you for letting me share my Seoul.

같이 가자!

Sincerely,
Taryn Blake

---

[2] No seriously. Look it up. My favorite year was 2009 when someone blocked a door with a couch? A mattress? lol

# Essays

한국에 어서오세요!

# Through the Looking-Glass

Korea's Incheon Airport is massive. Few other airports compare in size, quality, and efficiency. Incheon serves as the primary airport for an entire nation of 50 million people.

That's more people than Canada—in a space the size of Kentucky.

At all times of the day and night, there are gaggles of people outside the international arrival doors. Family members, business personnel, and unauthorized taxi drivers compete for the best view and the most space.

Occasionally, security has to enforce respect for the entryways.

This was one of those days.

The bright summer sun shone down through three-story-high glass walls into a vast ground floor foyer.

As I exited the customs area, I was greeted with a sea of clamoring faces. I navigated past the waiting crowd with an increasing sense that I had no idea where I was.

*Dunkin Donuts.*

*Paris Baguette.*

*Gifts.*

*Souvenirs.*

All the shops in my line of sight were unexpectedly titled in English or French.

I pushed my luggage cart further into the looking glass...

"Are you a teacher?"

I turned my head to identify the source of the question and saw a wall of Asian faces. I'm pretty sure I was wearing my default *paranoid-urbanite-being-addressed-by-a-stranger face.* [1] The girl who questioned me seemed oblivious to it. She was staring right at me, her luggage cart piled every bit as high as my own.

"Yeah, I am. How did you know?" I replied.

"You don't look military. Did you come with S.M.O.E.?"

---

[1] By now, I'm sure everyone has seen the movie *Taken (2008)*. My attitude was not unwarranted thank you very much! Fun fact: There's a Korean film called *The Man from Nowhere* (아저씨, 2010) with a somewhat similar plot but way more violence.

"Yeah." I now began to wonder if I was being hustled.

"I did too. We're supposed to meet at Arrival Gate F," the girl assures me.

Fourteen hours stuffed onto the plane and I didn't have the sense to find out what to do *after* I walked through customs. I was so flustered about (this) my first international trip, that I expended what little energy I had left, after nearly three days of only three hours sleep, figuring out whether I had filled out the arrival and entry cards correctly.

This was energy poorly spent because I was now in the hands of a complete stranger, walking to a destination I knew nothing about.

But why not? I had come to Korea for adventure.

I followed this girl—Liz Kang, from Orange County, as she had introduced herself—to the furthest end of the arrivals foyer. There was indeed a seating area populated with a couple dozen mostly 20-somethings of various nationalities. I was relieved to see a few other brown faces.

We gave each other barely perceptible *What's up?* head nods in acknowledgement. *That is what's up. Black people doing their thing in Asia! I'm glad to see y'all. I wonder if she knows where I can get my hair done—*

My reverie was interrupted by a Seoul Metropolitan Office of Education staff member asking for my name. To preempt any confusion from the inexplicable complexity of spelling a word that foolishly uses "y" as a vowel in the middle rather than the end, I spelled out my first name.

"You are not on the list," a young Korean woman told me.

"Are you sure?" Liz asked, annoyed on my behalf. Her voice betrayed years of practicing this dialogue outside nightclubs in Koreatown, Los Angeles.[2]

The girl became mildly flustered—an expression I would encounter about twice daily during my stay in-country—then walked over to talk with another staff member.

I was off to a wonderful start.

"Maybe it's because I missed my flight yesterday?" I mused out loud.

The girl returned with a male staffer, no older than 30.

"Heyyy," he said by way of introduction. "She said your name's not on the list?"

"Yeah," I confirmed.

"Well, she missed her flight," Liz interjected. "Is that why?"

"Oh, yeahhh. Probably," he replied. He said something to the girl in Korean and she walked off. "You're here for S.M.O.E., right?"

"Yeah."

"You're probably on yesterday's list. Nobody told

---

[2] If you're unaware how they get down out there, check out the pilot episode of *K-Town*, the show no one asked for, but a great many people passionately discussed.

us you were coming today..." his voice trailed off as he took in Liz's facial expression. It exuded both, *Don't bullshit me* and *I knew you were going to eff.you.see.kay. things up* at the same time—because you did these two things if you saw her make this face.

"Don't worry about it," he said. "We'll get everything figured out at the retreat center. The bus is on its way."

The staffer hardly made it 10 feet away before Liz blurted out:

"*Ugh*. Everything here is *so* disorganized!"

In retrospect, I'd say things in Korea aren't so much "disorganized" as they are simply subject to a unique organizational system that defies external scrutiny or justification. You know... "cultural differences."

❀❀❀❀❀

Before we proceed, let's go back to that missed flight. It's symbolic of an entire decade of misses in my life that preceded Korea.

I decided to leave the US because I turned 30 and realized I hadn't done any of the things that I had it in my head to do, so I decided to do them one at a time, starting with living overseas.

Graduating with an undergrad degree in journalism and public relations seemed like a safe bet after surviving Y2K back in 2000.[3] Unfortunately, I quickly realized I had no intention of becoming a spin doctor.

I had gotten a passport my senior year of college when a friend agreed to take a backpacking trip across Europe with me—then bailed.

Then I did a semester of film school back when this meant you had to learn how to load film into a camera for your future thesis project, but all the First Years were shooting on DV cassettes. At film school, I realized I had no intention of working in film production so I went back to journalism and public relations.

Time and money wasted.

Even though I'd had a passport for eight years, other than my Korean employment visa affixed firmly to an entire page of my booklet, every other page was still blank. I did not want my passport to expire in such a sorry state.

And this is how I chose Korea: One of my regular commenters on the Bollywood blog I was writing suggested that I watch a Korean drama that was similar to one of my beloved Indian films.

I watched said drama and was very intrigued. I googled other Korean programs and the most popular pop music. It was amazing.

Even though I had been self-studying Mandarin

---

[3] If you do not know what Y2K means, I'm probably old enough to be your mom. I'm not sure how either of us should feel about that.

for years, I chose Korea. I decided to spend a year in the media capital of Asia?

After years of crappy jobs outside my field, I had worked *in* my field for a total of three years and managed to ascend to a total salary of $30,000.

And this is how I quit my job: I told my boss I was going to spend the summer studying screenwriting in Los Angeles. He asked why I needed to quit because this was a non-profit and he could pick up the slack for a few months until I got back and he was really hoping that I would stay since he felt unsupported by other colleagues. *#officepolitics*

I told my boss I definitely wasn't coming back.

I believed that screenwriting was going to be The Thing and that Korea was going to be The Place. I would get my script finished and head back to LA to reconnect with my newfound contacts. Who knew? Maybe I'd even make media contacts in Korea.

What I knew for sure was that I would be teaching and that was all. What grade would I teach? Where would I live? How on earth would I make friends? But it didn't matter.

What I also knew was that the exchange rate was favorable—the Korean won was worth more than the US dollar. My vacation would equal to about 6 weeks a year. My employment package included a paid apartment and cash for a round trip flight back home each year.

Including my salary, the value exceeded my paltry nonprofit pay by a bit more than $10,000 dollars.

I would use the extra income to pay down my credit card debt. I would be able to pay off the few thousand left on my car note.

I might even send Sallie Mae a few bones for the first and the second time I went to grad school and quit. I could return to the US consumer-debt free!

Moment of silence for my optimism in the summer of 2008...

I thought it would be a good idea to sleep as little as possible before my flight to Korea so I'd be likely to sleep for the 14 hours it would take to get from the US to Seoul. I finished packing my clothes in the wee hours of the morning before my Saturday flight. I stayed up late talking to my mother and double checking that I had all the necessary documents: passport, work contract, letter of employment.

With a wild assortment of happy, anxious thoughts, I'm packing and doing 11th hour shopping, and packing again and some more. And I've got this massive cardboard box that I've packed with a bunch of clothes because I don't have enough money to buy more than one piece of legit luggage and my Filipino friend told me that's how they take stuff back to Asia so ok, why not?

That Filipino friend was my ex that I was supposed to marry but I called it off six weeks before the wedding and now I'm going to finally start a life that's more exciting than what we had and doesn't remind me of him either. But I'm not thinking about that.[4] I'm thinking, *What else can fit in this bag?*

Thinking and packing. I fall into a near-sleep brought on by exhaustion about four hours before I need to leave for the airport. I wake up. Worrying and double-checking. I am excited and delirious with anticipation.

I leave my house with just enough time to arrive at the airport two hours in advance, yet I arrive only one-and-a-half hours in advance.

*Why is there so much traffic on a Saturday?!*

My mother insists on parking the car to help accompany me to check-in.

More minutes burned.

I get to the airport counter and in front of me are a group of nearly 20 teenagers, a couple of chaperones, and only one counter agent. *Just, wow.*

---

[4] I promise, the story of my ex will be the next memoir.

The agent can't get them all on the same plane because of something that makes little sense, which means she needs more time to check and double check and there is no express lane at the airport.

By the time the woman has settled the group and issued their appropriate boarding passes for a completely different flight, I hope what little patience I have left will not be tested.

She pulls up my flight information.

"Let me see your orders."

"What do you mean?"

"You can't take a one-way flight if you don't have orders."

"Wha—? I'm not in the military. I'm working in Korea."

She looks at me like I am making things up and she. does. not. have. time. for. this.

*Dang, sista-girl!*

"I have my employment contract right here," I say as I try to remember which zippered compartment I tucked it into.

"Let me see," the agent replies, with a tone I'd describe as *Yeah, right.*

She takes the 15-page document from my hands and walks through a door labeled, Employees Only.

An eternity passes.

She steps out of the room, back to the counter and hands me my paperwork.

"Ok well. You're still not going to be able to get on this flight. It's too late to check your bags."

Under normal circumstances, this subpar level of nonchalant, not-my-problem customer service would have made me super angry. Like, *why are you such a worthless human being* angry. Instead, I became very, very silent.

Zombie silent.

Flat line silent.

I am completely overwhelmed.

*I am supposed to be in another country, on another continent, within 24 hours to meet my employers. Who am I supposed to contact? What's the time difference again? I can't believe this—*

"...that's the best we can do." The airline agent had been talking to me. I had heard the important part.

"Tomorrow?"

"Yeah, 8 a.m. so you won't miss your connecting flight."

I gather my large cardboard box, my massive piece of luggage, and cart myself out of the airport with no idea how this is going to turn out.

For the love of God, I'm 30 years old and I can't even catch a flight on time.

✿ ✿ ✿ ✿ ✿

Teacher training was held in a vacuous retreat center in a remote suburb of Seoul. I had no way to gauge the distance between the airport and our destination as we travelled along in our tour bus. I only know it was surrounded by trees and the one thing in walking distance was a small gas station.

On the ride to the training compound, Liz Kang and I had discovered we were both 30. Her most tragically disappointing breakup had just occurred a few months ago. We both grew up with parents who dragged us to church. I still attended voluntarily. She didn't.

As we pulled up to the facility, it felt like college all over again. Bright-eyed young people greeted us with instructions on where to place our luggage. I asked one of them about a cart for my large shipping box.

"That's yours?" a thin, male staffer asked, eyes wide in surprise.

"Yeah. It's got all my clothes in it."

"I don't think we have a cart," he laughed nervously.

I dragged my 56" hard shell Samsonite out of the way and leaned into the bowels of the bus to tug my oversized box out of the storage area. The box was no less than 40 pounds and nearly the length of my entire arm down to my fingertips. I can only imagine what I looked like as I attempted to move it.

"I can carry it for you," the staffer offered. I saw what *he* looked like as he strained to lift the box and felt a tinge of guilt.

"I've never seen anyone arrive with a box," he said, its weight pressed into his spindly arms.

I watched him struggle up the gravel path to the entryway.

How was I supposed to know they weren't going to have any dollies available? I remember seeing something about an "orientation" but I assumed it was going to be a short meeting before we moved into our accommodations later in the day.

I had also assumed that there was a universal understanding of the word, "bed," that included the attribute: "soft."

The beds at the training center felt like high quality cardboard layered with a quarter-inch of quilted padding. I rate sleeping on a non-carpeted floor a 2 out of 10. This was twice as good as that—bringing the experience to a solid 4 out of 10.

Stomach sleeping was out of the question and my body completely rebuffed more than 10 minutes of attempted side sleeping on such an insufferably hard surface.

As previously mentioned, I hadn't had a proper night's sleep for two days before traveling to Korea. By 10 p.m. on the third day of training, jet lag and the anticipation of another night of poor sleep sent me into tears as I lay down. No amount of willpower could force my body to relax enough to fall into a proper sleep.

No childhood fable resonated with me so much as, "The Princess and the Pea." We are kindred spirits she and I.[5] Since childhood, I too have been so delicate that my body cannot fall to sleep on any hard or uneven surface. And yet, I found myself in a country, on the portion of a continent where stone beds are considered a luxury. Had I known this beforehand, my adventure might have ended before it started. Clearly, fate had other plans.

Speaking of plans, whoever thought it would be ok to overlook the fact that it was entirely possible that for many of the teachers, their first introduction to Korean food would occur during the orientation, and that serving overcooked cafeteria food hastily slopped onto melamine trays might not make the best impression—whoever that person is, I hope they're reading this description and never do that anyone again.

If one is not careful, the overuse of chili paste can quickly turn a Korean meal into a monochromatic montage.

Friends, no one in the cafeteria was careful.

This orientation "meeting" was a week long. This was probably because, against my assumption that everything would have been arranged prior to our arrival, the staff was still scrambling to complete

---

[5] A quick summary of the fable is available on Wikipedia if you don't know the story.

school assignments and apartment leases *after* we arrived.

Halfway through the week, discontent amongst our ranks was apparent.

"I heard from the first group that arrived..." Liz Kang began conspiratorially, "that nobody has their schools yet."

"I thought they said they were going to tell us on the last day," I offered, still full of faith in The System.

"No. Like, they haven't even decided who's going where."

*Oh, snap.* Our training group was around 200 teachers. That's *a lot* of deciding.

"We should go tell them to put us in the same school," Liz suggested.

By "we," I was pretty sure she meant, *Come with me while I tell them what to do,* because as previously mentioned Liz was from The O.C., and also used to getting her way.

And I figure, *Why not? We're fast friends by now and neither of us much cares for any of the younguns we've met so far.*

Liz had determined that the young guy from the airport was actually in charge of coordinating our training. She, I mean *we,* managed to track him down—ok, noticed him down a side hallway— between training sessions.

"Hey! John," Liz called out in a friendly tone, ensuring he'd be a jerk if he pretended not to see us as we approached.

"Heyyyy. You guys need something?" I could almost *hear* John's body stiffen. At this point, everybody wanted something: More information. Better food. Entertainment. (Soft beds!)

No one expected to be in an isolated, though well-manicured(!), countryside compound instead of traipsing the streets of Seoul by Day 3 of their itinerary.

A lot of the kyopo[6] kids in particular had the inside track from friends and family. They were definitely expecting to be drinking on the sidewalk and partying until 5 a.m. Minor mutinies brewed.

Liz and I were senior citizens compared to that crowd. We wanted job assurances and high-quality real estate.

"Can you make sure we get put in the same school?" Liz asked.

"There's only one teacher per school."

"Sorry. We didn't know that," I offered. "I'm sure a lot of people have been bothering you."

John sighed. "Look, a lot of people are asking for special assignments because they want this or that neighborhood. We have to put people in the schools that requested teachers."

---

[6] This is the word used to describe Koreans who grew up away from Korea, (similar to "NRI" in India).

I'm sure Liz and I both looked disappointed.

Our fates were returned to chance.

"Who are you guys again?"

"Liz Kang and Taryn Blake," Liz answered.

I wondered if we were about to be blacklisted. But that was that.

Weeks and weeks later, we found out the school assignments were a bit like a professional sports draft pick. Not only were teachers asking for certain neighborhoods, the schools were trying to make requests. Certain schools preferred women or men. Others wanted religious adherents. There were sly requests for certain ethnicities. All of this is forbidden as part of Korea's HR policies for government employment.

The quirky part of this is the fact that religious or otherwise ideologically-led schools can become part of the public school (tuition-free) system in Seoul.

In exchange for inclusion, they must be open to hiring all qualified applicants regardless of creed, and similarly, offer admission to all students who are willing to participate in the culture of the school.

Additionally, a great number of Korean schools are single sex. A soft-spoken Canadian friend of mine ended up at one of the rougher boys' high schools. I'm sure both she, and the school, would have preferred them receiving a male teacher but again, policies prohibit making such a request.

Which is all simply to say, requests were made in abundance but rarely honored.

The only other memorable part of training week were the workshops. There was a review of our teacher's contract and "cultural" seminars with trite comparisons between Eastern and Western habits, including a bullet point on chopsticks. *Sigh*.

There were a couple of seemingly useful sessions on teaching methods and a single session on the Korean alphabet and common Korean phrases. The workshops were otherwise unremarkable. [7]

At the end of training week, we were divided into groups of north, south, east, and west based on the location of our school. Liz and I were happy to discover we were both placed in a western district.

In fact, we were placed in sister schools that shared the same athletic field.

Our studio apartments were on the same floor of the same building.

My school was a Christian school and Liz's was secular.

John hadn't asked about that part, but God got it exactly right.

---

[7] These unfortunately proved to be completely useless once we were actually in the classroom since we were told <u>not</u> to teach using the textbooks because that's what the Korean teachers use, so we should come up with something else on our own. *I'm sorry, do other people have B.Ed.'s in Curriculum? 'Cuz I don't.* And the Korean session? I remembered nothing!

아저씨들

# YOLO

After learning how to say hello, in the first batch of words a learner of Korean is likely to pick up is the word *ajosshi*. This a catchall word to describe a middle-aged man. It can be the polite equivalent of, "Mr." or the dismissive companion to "that old dude." (Similarly, middle aged women are called, *ajumma*.)

A man becomes an ajosshi by getting married or aging sufficiently such that people assume he's married. Any guy over 30 is pretty much an ajosshi hovering in the decades-long pit stop before *halaboji*, which means grandfather.

The working-class ajosshi stereotype is a guy who demands his own way in nearly every situation and regularly—as in 4-5 nights a week—drinks hard, with varying degrees of ability to hold his liquor.

At the low end of the spectrum, this encompasses men doing every possible variation of a diagonally-directed march to their home of origin. This species can be observed any night of the week in Seoul, crumbled under the weight of biology into a subway corner or park bench.

There they will slumber unmolested until morning when they will shake the wrinkles out of their clothing—sometimes a two-piece suit!—and stumble into a café for an Americano on their way back to work.

They are a visual delight to the uninitiated.[1]

Now, as any sensible person knows, stereotypes are only 60% true. With that in mind, let me share a few of my most memorable ajosshi interactions.

One day during my first year in Seoul, I had taken a trip to the main shopping district in the center of the city. The area, Myeongdong, is always packed with people nearly shoulder to shoulder on the weekends. For whatever reason, on this particular day I was out shopping alone, which apparently served as sufficient reason for a wandering ajosshi to proffer an introduction.

I worked my way through the crowd, walking what felt like upstream, as I attempted to weave a path

---

[1] Or for some people, the thought of well-dressed men frat-boy drunk, is just... *shocking*. If you are indeed uninitiated, you're probably thinking, "But why though?" Sorry y'all. It just *is*. And no one in Seoul (or Tokyo—FYI, they're even worse!) pays it any mind.

between scores of trendy couples intent on walking while holding hands, because it's absolutely necessary to physically manifest the message: "Two are better than one," while shopping for matching t-shirts.

"Ahh...Hello." From behind me, his voice somehow cut through the cacophony of chatter mixed with the shouts of salespeople and music blasting from every store.

Naturally, I ignored him.

I did this for two reasons: Anybody with a foreign face in Asia has people shouting "Hello!" (and nothing more) at them all times of the day and night. I was— and am—*so* over it. Secondly, I avoid talking to strangers unless it's absolutely necessary. Nothing personal.

If there's one thing you have to understand about ajosshis, is that when they're dealing with foreigners, they feel like they've got little to lose and everything to prove. Which is to say, the next time I heard his voice, he was standing right next to me.

"Hello!" He grinned.

"Hi." I gave a plastic smile without breaking my stride.

"Where ah you from?" his voice was a bit strained. He was on the chubby side. I suppose catching up to me had required more effort than he anticipated.

"America." I still had another 1,000 feet to the station. If there weren't so many people in the way, I definitely could've out-walked that guy.

"Ohhh. America, good. I like America."

*Congratulations?*

"Ah you solo?"

He got me. That question did not compute.

I had to stop walking because my brain couldn't figure out what he meant *and* use the resources necessary to communicate movement to my legs.

"What?"

"Ah you solo?"

Part of me wanted to say, *How did you know?! After Destiny's Child, I never thought I'd sing again but my album comes out next week!*

Instead, the confused scowl on my face induced babbling in my momentary companion.

"You... Do you have a boyfriend-uh?

*Aww hell naw.* I completely fell for the okey-doke.

"Yes," I said in the overly enunciated, crisp tone I use when completely lying. I punctuated the word with an affirmative head nod for good measure.

"Oh. You ah not solo."

"Nope. Sorry. Nice to meet you," I added with a cheery affectation as I resumed my pace. I chuckled and shook my head as I walked off. The amount of effort was flattering.

✱✱✱✱✱

Despite its small size, Korea has just as many cultural differences in its various regions as the

United States. Southern provinces have different pronunciation and occasionally, completely different vocabulary words that can't be found in any standard dictionary.

Where the men of Seoul, in the north, are generally thin and more often than not smartly dressed, the men of Busan, the southernmost city on the peninsula, are often tan and tattooed.

Without fail, there is an entire community of Busan men who spend the winter months in the gym awaiting beach season, when they break out their speedos and show off the fruits of their labor.

Busan has the most popular beach area in Korea and judging by the crowds during high season, it looks as if half the country goes there on any given weekend.

Haeundae Beach[2], the most popular of the two oceanfront areas, is always full of umbrellas clustered tip-to-tip as far as the eye can see. I grew up near the Atlantic Ocean and I'd never seen anything like it before Korea.

People come all the way from the city to the beach, then sit under umbrellas without ever soaking in the sun. Well, most people.

There's always a 20-foot-wide break in the infinite line of umbrellas that is full of "foreigners" lying out

---

[2] If you want to see what Haeundae looks like, watch the 2009 disaster film _Tidal Wave_ (해운대). Be forewarned, like all Korean films, it's just a matter of time before they kill your favorite characters.

trying to get a tan because that's what white-skinned people are supposed to do.

As for me, I always end up in that section because I'm usually with white-skinned friends and I refuse to pay to rent an umbrella.[3]

Having spent most of my life in cities near the ocean, Busan felt like home. On this trip to Busan, I travelled with my black American friend Izzy and my toy poodle Peppero.[4] The three of us spent the day on Haeundae beach checking out the local boys' tans and tattoos.

After nightfall, we headed over to Gwangalli, an oceanfront area famous for a bridge off the coast, lit with multicolored lights. All the high-rises facing the ocean are filled with bars, restaurants, cafes, and karaoke spots. The sides of the buildings are littered with bright neon signs naming every place inside.

Unlike Seoul, where nightlife is strictly segregated by age, the beach offers a little something for everyone in one place. It was there, in this milieu, that I encountered a unique species of middle-aged man I will simply call, Busan Ajosshi. This ajosshi not only had an approach, this man had a plan.

---

[3] Why on earth would you rent an umbrella when you could just go to the beach at 5 p.m.? It's far cooler in the afternoon and all the white-skinned people are usually packing up which leaves all the best spots on the shore open right around that time.

[4] Cutest and best dog ever! Named for the Korean version of Pocky called, Pepero (빼빼로). ^__^

While Izzy went to grab something from a convenience store, I chose to sit and wait for her across the street rather than attempt to sneak Peppero into yet another establishment. Izzy hadn't made it completely across the road before Busan Ajosshi approached.

"Hello."

This guy was definitely old enough to be my father. I gazed at him, from where I sat, waiting for his follow up speech.

"Where ah you from?"

I told him "America" as I tugged the leash of my always-too-friendly-at-all-the-wrong-moments poodle to keep her away from the man's feet.

"Do you live in Busahn?"

"No. I live in Seoul," I answered, sneaking a glance to the convenience store where Izzy was no. where. in. sight.

"Come. Have a durink wit me." *He's a forward one, isn't he?*

Too bad I don't bar hop with strange old men I met on the street.

"I'm waiting for my friend."

"Yes. She is going to the store."

*The Players Rulebook*, page 1: "Do not admit to women that you have knowledge of their situation that they didn't tell you themselves. This might be construed as stalking."

Seriously.

Busan Ajosshi chattered on while I gave polite grunts of affirmation.

It was the longest five minutes *ever* before Izzy came out of the store and headed back to where I sat.

As she got closer we made eye contact or rather, she made a face that said, "*Eww. What's going on?*" and I made an, "*I know, right?*" face.

"Hey, I'm back," she said as she approached.

Busan Ajosshi looked excited. *Two brown-skinned girls for the price of one!*

"Let's get durinks togetha."

"No. I have the dog. I can't take her anywhere."

"Yeah. We already made plans with my friend," Izzy said, giving Busan Ajosshi the stink eye. "Come on, let's go."

I stood up, offered Busan Ajosshi a forced and quickly faded smile. He looked a bit crestfallen. *Not tonight, buddy.*

"You're too nice," Izzy chided me as we walked away. "That's why he stayed around."

"It was awkward," I said. But really, I thought it might make a good story someday.

❀ ❀ ❀ ❀ ❀

Many of my most memorable ajosshi moments were forged in the salsa clubs of Seoul. There's no reason anyone would guess it, but the city has a vibrant partnered dance scene. Swing was the most popular dance among Koreans with salsa coming in at a close second. The swing dancing crowd tends to be younger, college to late 20's, while the salsa crowd is about the same age as your mom and her friends, no matter what decade she was born.

Some clubs are ageist, permitting only patrons 30-something and under—*starter ajosshis only, thank you very much*—while others cater to the older folks.

My favorite club was called, "Macondo," located in Hongdae, a neighborhood known for dance clubs, bars, and cafes catering to the college crowd.

Macondo was a place where all ages mixed freely. The music was a legit mix of salsa, bachata, and merengue: heavy on the salsa, no reggaeton. Just how I like it.

All of it was bodega music—none of that show tune stuff the Koreans in fancy Gangnam clubs play.[5]

In the back corner of the room there were bongos, a stray set of maracas and a couple of other indigenous percussive tools with even less English-sounding names. On weekends, the non-dancers could contribute to the merriment from the corners of the room.

For a season, I attended dance class there on a weekly basis. For about $6 USD, you got a dance

---

[5] For what my non-Latina opinion is worth, anything labeled, "Ballroom Salsa," is gonna be terrible. You want a playlist made by somebody's Puerto Rican uncle. Basically, start with Marc Anthony's "Vivir Mi Vida," and work your way up.

lesson *and* a free drink. My time was never wasted. Besides the physical exercise of dancing the night away, the people-watching was worth every penny.

One of the advanced class instructors went by the name Nirvana, because well, truth is far more fabulous than fiction. He was tall, had a mustache, a ponytail, and wavy hair: none of which come to mind where the word, "ajosshi" is concerned. Nirvana was clearly creating his own reality in this lifetime.

Despite being a larger man, Nirvana was as fleet-footed as any rooster released into a henhouse of middle-aged females seeking to revitalize their lives. Nirvana shimmied and swayed at Macondo nearly every Saturday, passing housewife after housewife across his arms.

On Saturday nights, the tiny dance floor of the basement club would fill far beyond fire code capacity. Around 12 a.m. or 1, the crowd would thicken to a nearly unbearable level. It was impossible not to bump other couples going into or out of a turn.

On the plus side, there's no room for any of that showy ballroom-dance-type salsa with "arm flairs" and excessive head flicks.

Staying close to your partner was a necessity.

One Saturday night, Izzy and I decided to stop in Macondo after clubbing elsewhere. The place was packed as usual and as it so happened, Nirvana was dancing not far from the entrance—probably so he could check out everybody who came in. No sooner had we hung our coats, than the current song ended, and Nirvana approached Izzy for a dance.

"I don't really know how to do salsa," she warned him. She told him she only knew the basic step and proceeded to demonstrate it for him.

"Let me teach you," Nirvana purred as he scooped her into his arms.

I watched as his palm slid down her curves to her lower back and his face lit up with delight. He used his other hand to signal a right turn. Izzy executed it successfully. Her face glowed with accomplishment. Nirvana's face shown with the delight of an old master securing the admiration of yet another young inexperienced pupil. Some ajosshi do have game.

My reverie on this sight was interrupted by one of my absolute least favorite dance partners—a guy I'll call Stumpy Ajosshi. The guy was short but strong. His hands were almost as big as his little head. Stumpy Ajosshi was determined.

I knew him from the weekly dance lessons. He came week after week but still lacked even an ounce of the sexiness salsa is known for. Heck, he didn't even look like he was having fun.

His hips looked like they were being pushed mechanically in and out of joint as he stomped, flat-footedly abusing the rhythms of salsa ballad after ballad.

Here's me being "too nice" again: I see Stumpy Ajosshi with his hand outstretched and think, *Even though he sucks, I should dance with him at least once.* I take his hand, and 60 seconds later I'm inwardly berating myself. We've already collided not only with each other but with the couple next to us.

And this...*this* is why I hate Stumpy Ajosshi, to counteract the embarrassment of what has just occurred, he starts doing an eight-count *out loud*.

"Wan." *Stomp!*

"To." *Stomp!*

"Tuhree." *Stomp!*

"An fo." *Stomp!*

The second time he gets to "two," he sends me into a right-hand turn. It goes ok, so on the next eight-count he has delusions of grandeur and tries to send me into a double turn. He sends me about one foot further from him than either of us can afford.

I graze the female partner of the couple behind us. She manages to sneak me a menacing snarl in between twirls. Stumpy Ajosshi overcompensates for the near disaster by yanking me forward.

He decides he will keep me close for the next three eight-counts by doing a series of basic eights and a sidestep.

*Stomp!* Yank. *Stomp!*

*Stomp!* Yank. *Stomp!*

*God. My wrists.*

Even my alleged niceness can no longer force a smile.

After another ill-advised turn, I notice my friends

across the room. They are enjoying the sight of this disaster far, far too much.

I take a look at Stumpy Ajosshi's face. His brow is furrowed in a fury of concentration; his lips puckered.

I laugh.

He notices. And thinks I'm enjoying myself.

I have failed.

And then, as suddenly as the end of the final pestilence God sent against Egypt in the Old Testament, the song ends and I too am free.

Stumpy Ajosshi wants to dance again but the end of a song is the "nicest" excuse to stop dancing.

❋ ❋ ❋ ❋ ❋

One of the notable things about Seoul is how there are generally many more taxis than are necessary clogging up the roads and canvassing for passengers. That is, until a person actually needs a taxi.

The trains in Seoul stop running between 12:30 and 1:30 a.m. depending on the night of the week. And depending on where you find yourself that time of night, it could take up to an hour to get a taxi.

There are two primary situations that fuel this phenomenon: 1) unpreparedness, and 2) grumpy ajosshi. The first situation can take anyone unawares if they aren't careful.

Let me explain.

You travel to a new area of town for some friend of

a friend's birthday party. Since this person isn't your *real* friend, you decline to head to the *noraebang*[6] for a round of karaoke, heading for the subway at 11:30 p.m.

Too bad in this round of *Choose Your Own Adventure* you've made the wrong choice. You checked the subway app on your phone to make sure there was an 11:30 train but you forgot to see if the train would actually go all the way to the end of the line instead of stopping God-knows-where on the wrong side of Seoul forcing everyone off into the dark of night.

You were so busy checking Facebook on your phone that you were genuinely startled when the train stopped only 15 minutes after you got on. *Blah blah blah something-issumnida*, you hear on the intercom as you watch everyone get off the train.

Someone is even nice enough to tap the drunk guy across from you to wake him. You leave the train, steering clear of Stumbling Drunk Man, and notice a few young guys bounding up the stairs. A couple of ajosshi run up behind them.

You look over your shoulder to make sure no one's chasing.

*What's the rush?* you wonder.

As you make your way to the street from the entryway of the stairs, between the bodies of the crowd that you have ascended and descended the

---

[6] This word literally means, "singing room." <u>It's sooo fun</u>! Just go!

stairs with, you see one of the Running Young Guys jump into a taxi.

One of the ajosshis jogs across the six-lane street just in time to catch a taxi going the other direction.

They are the lucky ones.

A gaggle of people stand on the opposite corner of the intersection with arms outstretched in hopes of attracting an empty cab. Most of the cabs passing by are already full. You move closer to the curb and crane your neck to get a view of the traffic coming your way.

There are few cars on the road in this corner of town but—*WHOOSH!!!* The tailwind of a passing bus swirls around your face and neck.

The bus stops just beyond you where a cluster of people materialize to board it. You look through the windows of the bus as it takes off.

Standing room only.

*Thanks, but no thanks,* you think.

Even if you wanted to take the bus, you wouldn't know which one to take. You've never been here before because it's the middle of No Place Interesting. Even with the city bus app you have on your phone, getting from No Place to home is harder than just clicking your heels together.

So you wait.

There's some logic to this system of getting a taxi: The driver stops for the person who's nearest the corner of the street.

Unless they don't.

Or unless some ajosshi and his mistress jump out in front of you at the last moment and steal your cab and you really want to curse them and/or punch them because it's been 30 minutes already and they totally saw you standing there because the woman looked over her shoulder for godssake before she jumped in the cab.

You can curse them if you like, but you can't punch them because they've already sped away.

You call a translation service to call a cab company for you because it's 2010, so there's not "an app for that" yet, *and seriously, it's almost 1 a.m.,* and you're standing on the corner in your club clothes like a hooker after all your mother's admonishment about not being "out running the streets."

The lady at the cab service asks where you are. You have no idea but read the street sign in your best Korean and describe the rundown shopping center across the street.

*We don't have anyone close to there,* she tells you, if she even understands where exactly you are because her English isn't that stellar and your Korean isn't either. *Why don't you just wait? I'm sure a taxi will come by.* The only thing you're sure of is that you wasted precious minutes on this cellphone call.

Ultimately, you will search the bus app and hop into an overcrowded bus and another bus and walk the last mile to your residence, arriving an hour and a half after you first left the train in which case you should've just gone to a round of karaoke.

In scenario two, you did your due diligence. You decided you were party rockin'. You went to the cool part of town with your crew and partied until all the alcohol-free establishments closed down.

You're in Itaewon, Hongdae, or Gangnam looking like a rock star but your feet are crying for freedom from the tyranny of the shoes you've inflicted on them.

You wave down a taxi.

*Where are you going?* asks the driver.

You sense his impatience and tell him the name of your neighborhood in your best Korean but because it's not even a fraction as busy and happening as the place you are right now, he tells you, *No.*

Or maybe he just makes an angry grunt and speeds off because grumpy ajosshi can't be bothered to respond to questions they don't like.

Never mind that the man is sitting in a taxi that says "vacant," he doesn't like where you live and he's not going, dammit.

The second time this happens, you take it a bit personally. *Is it because I'm black/a foreigner/speak crappy Korean?* you wonder.

Then you notice other people, mostly locals, in various stages of inebriation, flowing from taxi to taxi like bees collecting nectar, the result of which is far less sweet.

They flag down taxis. They approach the taxis parked near the curb. They are trying to find someone to take them home but the grumpy ajosshi are refusing.

You realize for some ridiculous reason, your odds of getting a taxi to your neighborhood are about 1 in 4. And after the time you and your friends pound the pavement in ill-fitting, yet appropriately glamorous heels for so long that you nearly break into tears while praying to Jesus *out loud* for a way to get home, you will always hit the club with a purse big enough to fit a pair of ballet flats inside.

❋ ❋ ❋ ❋ ❋

After another long night out, Izzy and I said goodbye to our friends and took on the challenge of hailing a taxi back to our side of town. We were leaving Itaewon, Seoul's most famous foreigner neighborhood. We headed to the less crowded end of the street and fortunately, were picked up by the second taxi we tried to hail.

The cab pulled over with speedy efficiency and we hopped inside.

"Oh, wow," one or both of us said as we were greeted with the sound of "*next thing you know, shawty got low, low, low, low...*" coming from the car speakers.

"Where are you going?" the driver asked.

As Izzy answered him, I took a moment to recover

from the sounds of T-Pain's greatest hits and absorb what I was seeing. Our driver had on a puffer jacket with fur trim on the hood.

The stereo system was backlit with multicolor LED lights that appeared to chase one another in laps around the perimeter of the radio.

I settled into my seat as the driver sped off. As if in slow motion, my mind absorbed the fact that the roof of the car was upholstered with red pleather.

*Red pleather!* It was fixed with matching red-pleather-covered "buttons" the size of a quarter. The sound of the driver's voice interrupted my thoughts—

"Where ah you from?"

I let Izzy answer. I was still trying to piece together the fragments of my brain from the blowing of my mind that had occurred a few seconds earlier.

"Ahh. I love America. My brotha lives there. I will move there next-uh year."

"That's cool that you love America," Izzy encouraged him.

"Yes. And I really love hip hop-uh. Do you know this-uh song?"

Taxi Ajosshi pressed a button on the stereo. A new beat dropped, then: "*She moves her body like a cyclooooone...* "Unfortunately, I do know this song. It's super catchy and it played virtually everywhere the summer of '07.

"Cyclooooone," Taxi Ajosshi sang along.

Izzy and I both giggled.

Taxi Ajosshi laughed too.

"You really like this song!" Izzy said.

"Yes. I like-uh this rap, T-Pain."

We both laughed again. This was definitely not a typical ajosshi we were dealing with.

"I like your car," I told him. "It's really *different*."

"Thank you. I did it myself."

"Really?!" asked Isi. "It looks really good!"

"I will work on cars with-uh my brotha when I go to L.A."

I really hope Taxi Ajosshi made it to Los Angeles. I can't help but wish good vibes on somebody who so clearly lives life his own colorful way. He's probably there pimping out people's hip hop rides for a living, while singing T-Pain songs, which is so wrong, but so absolutely right.

After all, you only live once. #*YOLO*

찜질방

# Naked and Afraid

Maybe it was the disorientation of the leisurely post-ark-building life, maybe it was having lost all his childhood friends in The Flood, but the old Biblical patriarch Noah had gotten to the place where he couldn't hold his liquor.

He made a batch of the good stuff, drank it, ended up buck-naked and passed the hell out. His son Ham saw the spectacle and called his two brothers over to get a laugh.

His brothers were pretty mortified and decided to take Dad some clothes. They carried them *backwards* so they wouldn't see his body and dropped the clothes over his "nakedness" to cover him up.

When Noah woke up and found out what had happened, he cursed Ham's fourth son, Canaan.[1]

The story has a lot of gaps. (I mean, was Canaan even there?!) Nevertheless, as a child raised on the religious tradition of fear mongering, I caught the important parts: 1) Don't be looking at people's "nakedness" and, 2) If you get drunk, you're gonna wake up naked. (For the record, these two life lessons successfully carried me from childhood to my 20's.)

Fast forward: When I first heard of a "public bath," it was in the context of the Roman Empire or maybe the ancient Greeks. Does it matter which? Both civilizations were likely driven to obscurity by the immorality of "public baths."

The idea that such places still existed was a shock to me when I heard about them in my late teens but I was led to believe they were only in Japan, a far, far off land where people couldn't possibly know better—*bless their hearts*.

When one of my university professors mentioned Bette Midler singing in gay bathhouses in New York, I had a vision of a roomful of people listening to schmaltzy ballads in their birthday suits. *Thanks for the invite, but I'm good.*

To an introvert, having unwanted people in "your space" borders on offensive. To me, the idea of having unwanted people in my space while naked is

---

[1] This story can be found in <u>Genesis chapter 9, verses 18-27</u> if you're interested!

downright traumatizing.

In most of Asia, bathtubs are a luxury not easily found. Korea is no exception. Thus, a shower-only lifestyle is easily mitigated by a trip to the local bath for relaxation—or family fun and frolic. Yes, it is true: Asia's public baths are bastions of intergenerational nakedness.[2]

I understand that not all readers share my aversions. It is simply that, Biblical symbolism aside, a person needs to develop a neutral feeling toward jumping into the bath with Grandma rather early in life to find it innocuous, and clearly, my time for the formation of such sentiments has passed.

When I learned about the culture of public baths in Korea—*jim-jil-bahng*—in the native tongue, I vowed, due to generally inescapable lapses of public decorum, not to place my beloved bare body in the metaphorical hands of the collective Korean trust.

There are more examples than are worth explaining why I had no reason to believe that the locals' penchant for pointing and shouting, "Wow! A foreigner!" as I passed by would be abated by the particulars of public nudity.

In fact, I was worried that the allure of my smoothly curved cocoa brown bootyliciousness might be too much for the more vocal ajummas to resist.

---

[2] In Japan, they even have co-ed nude saunas! *#doubleNoThanks!*

One need only hear, "You, body, good," from a stranger so many times before it becomes, well, strange.

The topic of Korean saunas often came up with fellow teachers, many of whom enjoyed regular visits to neighborhood baths.

"I had such a tough week, I stopped by the jjimjilbang on the way home..." someone would start, while each of us listened, knowingly anticipating a tale centered on the violation of one personal boundary or another. "...and I saw three of my students!"

"Were you in the pool?" someone asks. A "yes" will be greeted by shoulders shrugged in relief but "no" will bring a chorus of sympathy. Being naked and partially submerged is far better than standing exposed in the open while trying to maintain a façade of friendliness and professionalism.

How *does* one end a nude conversation with students? A hug is certainly out of the question.

For this element of Korean culture, the public bath, I figured, *To each his or her own.* Unless he or she is a teacher patronizing a neighborhood bath near his or her school. In that case, your recurring nightmare about appearing at work naked is completely justified.

The more harrowing tales typically involved older ajosshis and ajummas. As is common the world over, acquiring the rank of senior citizen frees one from the expectations of civility harnessed upon the young. In this, Korea is no exception.

If anything, deeply imbedded Confucianism has made elders more bold in their transgressions. "You, big-sizuh," a simple conversation starter; questions about the heaviness of one's supple breasts: mere girl talk; a stray eye affixed to one's manhood, followed by, "You, girlfriend, very happy," simply the most gratuitous affection one man could show another.

I failed to mention earlier that there is an additional element to my aversion that readers of African descent are probably surprised I haven't already discussed. Black people don't do group nakedness.

"The last time my friends and I went skinny dipping..." said no black man ever. It's just a rule. Because it makes perfectly good sense.

Nudism isn't a particularly sustainable lifestyle for the Great Outdoors. (See the television program *Naked and Afraid* for tangible evidence.)

Even for short stints, group nudity is one of the main reasons I have judiciously avoided both the military and prison.

So it was, in the face of these carefully defined and culturally undergirded personal boundaries, that I received the shock of a social invitation to a Korean sauna from Janelle, one of my black Christian friends.

After a year of avoiding this quintessential Korean experience, I was circumstantially badgered out of my objections.

"Who ever heard of black people sitting around

naked?" I asked, quite sensibly, to a table full of black women.

"I go all the time," Janelle answered in her typically cheery manner.

"It's so relaxing," another of the women named Opal opined.

*Right.*

*Public nudity : relaxing :: root canal : fun.*

"How can it be relaxing when there's a bunch of people in there? You know how Koreans are on the subway."

"It won't be crowded at 2 a.m."

Janelle lived in a small town, so her plan was to party in Seoul for her last night in Korea, spend the night at the jjimjilbang, then head to the airport. Oh yes, dear reader, the Korean sauna is not just a place for the public shedding of garments, you can also sleep there.

"So we're just gonna sit around naked, and then go to sleep?" I asked. I'm pretty sure I glared at each of them while squinting my eyes into little slits. *Do you not realize the absurdity of this proposal?* I scanned their faces for any sign of recognition.

"Well, they have a food café. We can get ice cream or something," one of them offered.

"You should come. It's my last night in Korea," said Janelle. Clearly, I wasn't getting through to them, nor out of joining them.

I surrendered.

Janelle was leaving Korea. If things went terribly awry, I'd simply call it the end of our friendship. As for the other girls, they were her friends, not mine. Better naked with strangers than with friends, right?

That way, it's like it never happened at all.

On that fateful evening, I piled out of a cab with the other girls and stood on the curb facing the massive three-part structure that houses Yongsan station.

The building holds a train and aboveground rail station, a large shopping center, a movie theater with IMAX, and a big box retailer. It is modern to the point of invoking the image of a space station. I assumed this was our destination.

"It's over there," Janelle said, noting my confusion.

*There* was a billboard-like sign with a large moving clock and multicolor digital tickertape below it. The sign read "Dragon Hill Spa" in Korean with a subtitle confirming it was a 24-hour sauna.

This banner was the entryway to a recessed area that is best described as a courtyard. On the right was a tall white building with about six-stories of façade attempting to channel Cesar's Palace casino. Also not our destination.

To the rear of the courtyard, there was a two-story building apparently staging a private Spanish

Colonial Revival: tan stucco walls, clay terracotta roof tiles, and an arched entry, but sadly, no actual dragons.

At the time, I didn't notice the illuminated statue of a larger-than-life nude woman, one arm across her abdomen, clutching her back, the other stretched taut to clasp her ankle.

Both arms force her bountiful breasts to spill outward as her head, tilted ever so slightly in rapture, causes her long tresses to cascade near her knee while she crouches with her buttocks planted firmly on a small cube.

I didn't notice it because that is Way Too Much.[3] Clearly the universe didn't want me ending this experience before it began.

Dragon Hill Spa is considered a "luxury jjimjilbang." This basically means that the place is huge, you can be sure that no homeless-looking people will be inside, and that the towels are monogramed.

We checked in at the counter along with three guy friends of Janelle's who had tagged along. We each paid our 12,000 won ($11) entry fee and passed through the turnstile of no return. The fellas walked to the men's area and we took the elevator to the women's area.

---

[3] Apparently, I wasn't the only person who thought so. The statue is still there but they've since hidden her off to the side (but you can see her in the Google Maps view.)

Things were about to get real.

✾ ✾ ✾ ✾ ✾

The locker room was brightly lit and appeared to be clean. I had hoped for full-size lockers so I would have a little sliver of metal to hide behind but to no avail. We four girls split up. Two of us on one row of lockers, the other two on the next row.

"I'll go over here," said Opal, my locker partner. On the way over, I had repeatedly reminded everyone how very much I needed my "personal space" seeing as how this was my first time and all. She was kind enough to remember.

"When do we get to put these on?" I asked, indicating the cotton shorts and matching tunic shirt that were provided by the spa.

"When we get ready to go upstairs," was the disappointing answer.

I attempted to wrap my body with the spa-provided towel but it absolutely refused to cover both my breasts and butt cheeks. In an exercise of futility, I held the towel over my chest lengthways. The bottom end lapped against my pelvis as I walked. I suddenly called all of my personal grooming habits into question.

*Why hadn't I thought about this beforehand?* Was there any hope for an evening that was going below the belt so quickly?

I trailed behind the other girls as we approached the main spa area. I quite literally brought up the rear. I reminded myself that if I just stayed calm, I'd probably remember none of this later on.

The things we tell ourselves...

The entryway to the main spa area is lined with showerheads flanked by 12" deep Plexiglas dividers. Since the dividers are 1) see-through and 2) more narrow than the "luxury" towels, they serve no real purpose other than to remind the people near you to stay on their own side. *Thank you jjimjilbang designer!*

After a night of clubbing, I was fresh with the fragrance of l'eau de smoky-booze-filled nightclub. I needed a shower. I wanted a shower. For the sake of my fellow humans with whom I would be sharing the pools, I had to shower. And shower I did. I used the little bar of travel soap I'd purchased at the front counter and did my duty.

Most of it.

In this already awkward moment of vulnerability, I offer full disclosure: I didn't fully launder my nooks and crannies. My naughty bits were still a tad naughty when I hit the pools.

Look, I wanted to fully participate in the social contract that is The Public Bath. I wanted my body to be as clean as humanly possible. Unfortunately, I have a very delicate and polite 2.5-step process by which I accomplish this under normal circumstances.

In public showers? Just... No.

As it stood, I was already trailing behind the other girls. I hosed down my underside and called it fair game. Off to the pools I went.

Janelle, Opal, and the other two girls were already sitting in one of the larger pools. They invited me in. I stepped down into the pool. It was *extra*-hot hot tub temperature. I dipped myself into the steamy water.

As the line of water slipped up my body to my neck, I felt my lungs contract under the influence of heat and steam. I was anything but relaxed.

"How is it?" Janelle asked.

"It's ok. I guess. At least there's nobody in here."

The room was massive, around the size of a small gymnasium. Lining the walls of the room were about six different baths each with seating for at least four people.

"Nobody" consisted of two middle-aged Korean ladies, a young Korean woman, and one cleaning ajumma. I had no complaints in this regard. *The fewer the merrier.*

I was just getting used to once again having a barrier between my body and the public when the drama queen of our squad squealed, "Let's try the cold pool!"

Her body appeared to explode out of the water as she popped up, full of excitement.

*Did she just say "cold pool"*?! Oh, the dread.

I watched as Drama Queen crossed the room to one of the other pools. I'm pretty sure the temperature reading next to it had a minus symbol in front of it.

She stepped down into the water. When her feet hit the bottom of the pool and the water hit her thighs, she squealed, then broke into a series of giggling shrieks and oh-my-gods. She stomped a couple of times in place before scrambling out of the pool.

Absolute shenanigans. All of us burst out laughing.

"Is it really that cold?" Janelle asked.

She walked over to the pool herself and stuck her foot in the water. Judging by the pitch of the screeching sound she made, the answer was clear.

"That's the coldest one," the veteran sauna goer, Opal, informed us. "You should do the cool one over there." At her advice, everyone headed to the warmer cold pool—degrees: zero. Shrieks and groans abounded.

I watched them from my seat in the hot pool, hardly able to breathe but far less excited about the prospect of freezing to death naked.

"You should do this one," Opal assured me. "The contrast of hot and cold is good for you."

She sounded like a brochure.

I stepped out of the hot pool, tiptoed across the wet stone floor as fast as I possibly could, and climbed into the cold pool.

"Oh my God!" I screamed. The contrast in temperature felt like prickly pins on my body. The look on my face sent the other girls into peals of laughter that ricocheted off the walls. There I stood in my birthday suit, too cold to sit down, too embarrassed to stand up.

*Why Lawd, why?!*

I put my body under the water and endured the shock. At least I could breathe again.

It felt as if I had only just sat down before someone mentioned we should try the outdoor pool. Personally, I felt as if I had seen enough to justify having "had" a jjimjilbang experience. It was late summer. The temperature outside would be 70°F at most.

"I'm already cold in here," I objected.

"The outside pool is warm," Janelle stated as she got up, grabbed her things, and to headed toward the door. The others began to follow. I realized I had left my towel near the warm pool. I stepped out of the cold water and went back to get it.

And then it happened.

I grabbed my towel and spun around. I began scurrying across the room to catch up and for no logically explicable reason Opal's body was positioned directly in front of me.

*BOOM!*

Flesh pressed against flesh in one eternally mortifying moment.

Time slowed.

Nay, *stopped.*

The space-time continuum condensed my fears

and reality into one irrevocable physical action. Somehow, we were going in opposite directions but didn't successfully make the "ships in the night" pass as I had envisioned.

"Uh, sorry," I muttered, barely conscious.

Mentally, I had retreated to my "safe space" to recover. This day's safe space was a sunny land of appropriately clothed people passing one another without bumping in a dry, non-humid environment. Everyone's hair looked amazing.

When I looked up, Opal was already exiting the door to the outdoor area. I grabbed my luxury towel. I had inadvertently dropped it on a puddle of water. It was soaked on one end. The knobby texture felt like sad, soggy oatmeal. I placed the oatmeal over my chest and dashed over to the doors. A blast of cool air met me on the other side.

The sky was the cloudless off-black of City Night. There are too many lights in Seoul for the sky to ever appear as the deep, dark expanse poetry is made of. There are no stars, just billions and billions of neon lights.

Despite the open view of the sky, we were truly not on the roof as I had supposed. A portion of the building extended in what appeared to be two additional stories on the sides of the pool opposite the entry doors. I scanned the roofline for peeping toms. I didn't see any but I wondered aloud how often they'd had to pull people down from the roof.

"Calm *down*," Drama Queen said as she splashed into the water and let out a loud squeal.

We all filed into the pool, vigorously exclaiming what a relief the warm water was against the cool air of the night.

The two middle-aged Korean ladies had been quietly conversing in the corner of the pool. After our boisterous entry, one of them said something to the other—judging by the stank face she threw our way, it was: "Oh my word, those young foreign girls are way too loud. Let's get out of here"—and they went back inside the building.

"I guess we pissed them off," Drama Queen giggled.

*The fewer the merrier.*

The outdoor pool was the least awful part of the sauna so far. The contrast between the cool night air and the warm water was pleasant.

In a bathing suit with a head of preconditioned hair, I'd likely have been relaxed enough to enjoy floating on the water while satellite-gazing into the night.

This was not that occasion. I kept my bare butt submerged and let my nerves unwind.

Somebody mentioned we should probably go meet the boys before they started wondering where we were. In my fright, I had forgotten all about them. I realized this meant we could go put on some clothes.

*I should have thought of that!* Except I really couldn't

have because I had no idea how this all worked. I would've filed that idea way for next time except I was quite certain there would be no "next time."

I followed the girls back inside the building. The stuffy, dank air of the sauna room was more shocking the second time. We trailed back through the stone floor room toward the locker area.

Around the corner, I noticed a small, unoccupied bamboo-paneled room. Along one wall was a stack of small brown ceramic pots with handles; on the other, a line of small brown stools. Each stool had a large, round hole in its center. I couldn't fathom what they were for.

On the glass panel that composed the outer wall of the room, the words, "Emperor Oriental Medicine Hip Washing" were printed underneath some large Korean writing and between two silhouettes of a phoenix/peacock hybrid animal.

On the window were taped price listings and a photo montage of several different colored herbs, two cups of tea, herbs in a ceramic pot and the *pièce de résistance*: a photo of two women, their heads wrapped in blue luxury towels, their bodies draped from neck to toe in pink shiny cloth not unlike a drape at the hair salon.

At the lower edges of the pink drape, the telltale outline of the low square stool could be seen. The women's placid expressions testified to the efficacy of the service.

The English price listing explained that the treatment was used to "deeply penetrate the womb and skin." After a year of living in Korea, I had warmed to the idea of the toilet seat bidet but this—this was far above any level of intervention I had ever imagined necessary.[4]

"What the heck is 'hip washing'?" I wondered aloud.

"They steam your vagina," Opal replied with an air of unaffected pragmatism. *The Korea Tourism Board should snatch this girl up for a promo commercial. Seriously.*

"Have you tried it?"

"Yeah. It's really refreshing. They steam your face at the same time."

No comment.

I walked back to the locker room and threw on the complementary shorts and shirt. I was back in my element. I had stared the jjimjilbang in the face and returned unscathed.

Emotionally unscathed anyway.

Well, except for that "bumping" incident.

---

[4] Later, when my Korean improved, I searched the internet for "hip washing" based on the Korean characters, 황실한방좌욕. Even though it uses steam, the phenomenon can be more properly translated to English as a "sitz bath." I find it problematic however, that the word "sitz" sounds so much like "Sith."

That is how I usually pronounce the word in my mind. After completely translating 황실한방좌욕 to "Imperial Oriental Medicinal Sitz Bath," my mind automatically transliterated it into "Imperial Overlord Maleficent Sith Bath" which as its name implies and any Star Wars fan can attest, would be very, very dangerous.

But I was physically unharmed.

I think.

They don't use any chlorine in those pools. I probably should have used the "hip washing" after all.

# You Gotta Have Faith

My friend Hannah's friend Joanna tells her about the New Church she's going to because her current boyfriend is friends with the pastor so they both left the church where they originally met.

"It's really good," she tells Hannah.

So Hannah tells me and I say, "cool," because the church where Joanna and her boyfriend originally met was the church that I originally went to in Korea until I stopped and now I'm not going anywhere.

It's not the fact that some of the most annoying kyopos[1] I know went to the Original Church. Or that one of the head ushers was a guy I saw at the club with a girl pushed up against the wall when I left at 2 a.m. who still beat me to church by several hours to greet

---

[1] In this case, Korean-Americans

64 BEARING MY SEOUL

me at the front door in the morning.

Or that it seemed to be the premiere destination for Korean guys who were seeking to *exclusively* date white women. Or Korean girls seeking a homeland tour that *only* included people who looked like the homeland.

Nah. None of those reasons.

I stopped going there because no one talked to me. As in, I'm telling this to a friend who suggests, "Join a small group," which I did, and then I was in a small room with a small group of people who were doubled up talking to each other while I stared at the wall and waited for the leader to start asking the questions on the piece of paper he's instructed to follow.

And repeat. For weeks.[2]

One Sunday, unprompted, the leader addressed me directly, (!) "How was your week?"

I told him the play-by-play about how a drunk guy tried to pull me onto the train Friday afternoon on my way home from work because well, that was the most poignant moment of my week.[3] He looked at

---

[2] Ok, actually, there was <u>one</u> kyopo girl in the small group who would always say, "Hi." I don't remember her name but I always enjoyed talking to her. I added this footnote just in case she reads this book. In case you're one of those social butterflies thinking, *Well, did you talk to <u>them</u>?* Look, I don't ignore people in social settings. I smile and I'll greet people but I don't jump in conversations I haven't been invited to. Stop victim blaming! lol

[3] For those of you who were concerned, it was an empty station except for me and the drunk guy... and a security guard. There is no

me flatly and said, "I apologize for my people," to which I replied, "My people thank you," because 1) this dude was Korean *American* so *What on earth are you talking about bro?* and 2) it's weird when people talk like robots. As this was my first real conversation with anyone in this group, I realized I would rather leave on a high note, so it would also be my last.

Unlike Original Church, which was located in an upscale, trendy area of Seoul, New Church was in a nondescript area of town up a steep hill that started after a five-minute bus ride from the nearest subway station. Whoever founded the church clearly hadn't considered what a poor marketing move that would be several decades later.

There Hannah and I are, said decades later, getting off the train and off the bus and it's 2009 so we have some directions on a scrap of paper but there still

---

reason to be close to THE ONLY OTHER PERSON in the subway station and keep moving forward when they back away.

I screamed at the drunk guy a couple of times to back up cuz he was being creepy and smelled like a bar room floor. I assumed he didn't understand English but everybody understands being yelled at.

When he grabbed me, I counterbalanced with my right leg and gave him a couple of quick kicks to the kneecap without spilling a single McDonald's french fry in the because you are not going waste my time AND my snacks.

After being kicked, the drunk guy got on the train. By himself.

I was definitely frazzled.

The security guy was a ridiculous waste of time. I saw him staring at me from the other end of the platform as I finished my french fries and waited for the next train.

Half of me wanted to scream at him too because, *Why are you looking at me after I secured myself?! Send me half your paycheck!*

aren't many street signs in less trafficked parts of Seoul.

Every part of the street looks similar to every other part of the street and there's no one to ask since we don't speak Korean and the ajummas and ajosshis in this part of town don't speak English.

We walk for 10 minutes, 20 minutes.

*Where are we supposed to cross the street?*

*This can't be right.*

*It's chilly outside.*

*Let's just go to a café.*

Mission aborted.

New Church would have to wait.

Until next week.


There Hannah and I are getting off the train and off the bus.

*We got off too early last time.*

*At least we got the right stop!*

*Ok, this is where we cross the street...right?*

It starts drizzling but we press on. Uphill. No sidewalk. Narrow street. *Is this right? It can't be right. Why are there no signs?! I can't believe we're out here getting rained on. We should get lunch instead.* We laugh it off. Mission aborted.

Until next week.

✺✺✺✺✺

I met Hannah my first week in Korea. She grew up in Tennessee and I lived there for seven years. Unlike me, Hannah has naturally blonde hair and grew up homeschooled. Like me, Hannah is a writer and intimately familiar with conservative strains of Christianity. We both came to Korea for Korea. We just "got" each other. Hannah was also the only person that would "get" my desire to make another attempt at visiting New Church. New Church wasn't like the controlling communities we had grown up in. It was "really good."

Take Three.

There Hannah and I are getting off the train an hour before service. There's a church shuttle bus. We hop on and are greeted by a friendly Korean American guy who introduces himself as Roy. He asks how we found the church, to which Hannah offers the short answer of, "my friend."

We three chat away as the shuttle rambles up the narrow roads to the church. Pedestrians keep out of the way as best they can between the passing mini-bus and parked cars that line the street. The area is largely residential and clearly working class. The apartment buildings are no higher than four stories each in every possible shade of brown brick and grey concrete.

The church bus hosts both youngish expats and some older Koreans headed to late service at the church. As we pull up to the building, we remark that we "would've *never* found this," which elicits a knowing chuckle from our guide. "Good thing you took the shuttle," he says with a smile.

The service isn't particularly memorable. Sound teaching. Charismatic preacher. Decent worship band.

As the service finishes, several folding tables worth of snacks have been set up in the foyer. Fresh fruit, sweet breads, and cups of juice are in neat lines on each one.

This is a wise choice. Nearly everyone flocks to the area as soon as the closing "amen" is spoken. Hannah and I are no exception.

As we hover near the edge of the gathering, a couple of regular attendees greet us. One is Anna, a bright-eyed Korean American girl who grew up in the Midwest. She has a sunny, open personality. I like her immediately.

"Is this your first time here?" she asks us. We confirm this is the case. "You guys should come eat! A bunch of us always go eat after church."

So we do.

And so begins the Sunday ritual I hold until leaving Korea.

❀ ❀ ❀ ❀ ❀

In the early days of New Church, it *was* really good. Every week before the sermon, someone would share a testimony of how their life had changed.

A good number of the stories involved how an exchange student came to Korea with the express purpose of clubbing, drinking and extensive sexipades but ran into some other kid on campus who introduced them to a completely new way of living.

There were stories of sibling and parent relationships restored, emotional healing, renewed life purpose—everything that made the idea of faith come alive.

New Church was the "English outreach" of the Korean church that chose the location on the top of the hill many decades ago. Unlike the parent church, the leadership of New Church was Korean American. Like the parent church, they were trained in the Presbyterian tradition.

By the time I had arrived at New Church, the congregation was in a stage of—in true Presbyterian style—studying everything they could possibly get their hands on about a new way of worshiping.

As the legend goes, two pastors ago, before I arrived at the church, they had invited an Argentinian guest speaker who introduced a gloriously wild strain of Pentecostalism.

Speaking in tongues? *Check*.

Fervent prayer? *Check*.

Weeping aloud? *Check*.

Prophecy? *Check*.

Healing? *Check*.

Fasting? *Check*.

I appeared somewhere around the end of this list and I was down for all of it.

A few weeks after I started attending, New Church invited another guest speaker from the US. This guy was a part of an "extreme prophetic" ministry. *#soextreme*

I had no idea what to expect but it didn't matter because what's life without a little skeptical excitement?

The experience was labeled as a Prophetic Activation. This consisted of a teaching on prophecy and "words of knowledge."[4] After a short prayer we broke into smaller groups and did prophetic exercises.

The first one I recall had to do with finding someone you didn't know and asking God to show you something about them. I sat across from a girl named Judy that I had never met before. *Better to mess up with a stranger, right?*

I closed my eyes to buy some time. I saw Judy. But not Judy!—an angelic amber lithograph of her face. Behind her shone a great and beautiful light. It brought tears to my eyes.

"Are you ok?" she asked.

"Judy, you're beautiful!" I sniffled. "You're glowing. It's like God is all over you. It's amazing."

---

[4] A "word of knowledge" is information that a person would have no way of knowing without supernatural assistance. Prophecy is the same except it concerns things that will happen in the future.

"Wow," she grinned, her eyes wide with wonder.

"You don't know Judy, right?" her overinvested friend questioned me. I replied in the negative.

"That's *exactly* how she is," she assured me.

*"Wow" is right.*

The last exercise of the night completely upped the ante. The group was split in two. Half of us stood in a line nearly shoulder to shoulder. (It was a small space.)

We were told to close our eyes. The other half of the group would step up in front of each one of us, one-on-one, and those with eyes closed would tell the person in front of them whatever word or prophecy they got.

I still remember the audible expressions of surprise and disbelief when we were told this. It makes me chuckle even now.

I was in the group that went first. I had some faith but not *that* much faith. With my eyes closed, I could feel my heart racing as someone stepped forward. I breathed a quick prayer then described each item as I saw it:

*An outdoor coliseum. An ancient one. Roman architecture. The seating area is full of people. The crowd is blurry.*

*There's light on the floor of the coliseum.*

*A man is walking out wearing armor. He's holding his sword up high.*

*The crowd is cheering... I think you're the gladiator.*

"I really hope you're a guy," I say as I open my eyes.

And in front of me, stood the most innocent-faced 21-year-old boy.

"Woaaahh," he said, tears forming at the corner of his eyes. "Thank you."

I was thankful everything came together so perfectly.

This is a good time for me to point out that none of the spiritual activity I've just described was foreign to me. By this time in my life, I'd experienced just about every mainstream Christian expression of worship and a couple of sketchier ones.

The significance of this experience was the fact that I wasn't watching things happen—I was doing them.

Historically, I'd been in services where people received prayer and fell down "in the Spirit." I'd receive the same prayer, by the same minister and be standing as tall as an oak tree.

Y'all, it is embarrassing when this happens.

In some ministries, if you're not out on the floor they assume it's because no one's prayed for you which means I get prayed for repeatedly if I'm anywhere near the altar.

I get it. It's not a good look to have that one person standing up in the sea of people laying down but I'm telling you, it's my birthright to be the last one standing.

Similarly, this prophetic activation evening

culminated with a time of ministry. Anyone who felt they needed prayer was invited to "come to the altar" so the guest speaker could pray over everyone.

Only haters hate prayer!

I went up front.

The speaker began working his way down the prayer line laying hands on each person as he went. Generally, this meant touching someone's head as he prayed. One of the church staff might also lay a hand on the person's shoulder and pray.

There were also a couple of "spotters"[5] just in case.

People definitely fell. I don't remember who or how because that's pretty much par for the course. I just remember the strange things, like people laughing uncontrollably while on the floor and one of the girls who couldn't seem to stop twirling in circles around the perimeter of the room. She mostly didn't bump into things either. Mostly.

I also remember what happened to me. How my body reacted to an extremely short prayer. As I recall it, the workshop host simply spoke the word, "love," three or four times with his hand lightly upon my head.

An intense warmth radiated through my body. Tears pushed to the corners of my eyes. I could not maintain my dignified stance of elbows at my side

---

[5] While "catchers" is more commonly used word, I generally prefer the word "spotters" which is more of a gymnastics/cheerleading reference because like Simone Biles, I don't be falling!

with lower arms and palms raised upwards.

My polite posture of prayer wilted as I began crying.

Ugly crying.

*This is how Claire Danes became famous* crying.

*This is how Viola Davis wins Oscars* crying.

*Public mourning in North Korea 'cuz Kim Jongil is dead and the camera is on* crying.

*Why doesn't anybody have a tissue?!* crying.

I bent over, arms stiff as my hands gripped my legs above the knee.

I sobbed. Probably wailed.

Each convulsion released a layer of heaviness weighing my soul. It was awkwardly amazing.

❀❀❀❀❀

During my second year in Korea, I was having terrible menstrual cramps that would react violently to an increasingly long list of food and drink that can best be summed up as caffeine, and anything that contained soy.

Y'all, everything in Korea contains soy.

The cramps would begin 3-5 days before my period, increase in intensity during my period, and let up 1-2 days afterwards. This was nearly two weeks a month of being scared to eat, taking up to the maximum daily dosage of ibuprofen, and some pretty heavy bleeding.

The ob/gyn told me the pain was because of fibroids. The clinic tech insisted that I look at them on screen as she poked the ultrasound wand in their direction. (#*canyounot*) The gyno showed me the fibroids on a printout of a grainy image that was supposed to be my uterine lining. They looked like orbs from a tabloid UFO-sighting photo and they felt like an alien invasion as my body attacked me at the slightest provocation.

During this season, a couple of staff from a 24-hour prayer ministry in the States paid a visit to New Church. This was the season in which the congregation was studying physical healing. A special evening service was held.

I was on pain killers the night of the service. In the bathroom before things started, I ran into my friend Rachel, a lovely brown-haired white girl from Oklahoma.

She made the mistake of asking how I was doing and I began rattling off a list of what I had eaten earlier in the day as I tried to discern the cause of the current round of cramps.

As always, Rachel's face radiated empathy. So much so that I felt bad for having burdened her. I apologized for rambling. She told me not to worry about it.

Inside the sanctuary, we sat with a few of our other friends. The sermon was a teaching on healing. The speakers shared testimonies from their experiences.

After service, people lined up for prayer—the usual.

Until a couple of people received immediate physical healings.

The atmosphere radiated with excitement.

Looks of surprise.

Tears of joy.

The worship band began to play again.

People sang and danced.


I observe the room around me fill with hope and joy. *I should ask someone to pray for my cramps*—the thought crosses my mind like a fleeting echo.

I doubt it.

*I've had cramps as long as I've had a period. Although the pain's gotten worse, it's a small thing. It's manageable, not life threatening.*

The second I finish this train of thought, Rachel appears in my periphery.

"We should pray for your cramps," she says confidently, eyes twinkling with energy.

"I just had that thought," I say, my eyes wide.

She grabs our friend Matt who is standing nearby.

"Taryn needs prayer," she says, grabbing his arm.

Another friend named Matt looks unoccupied. Rachel grabs him as well.

"Come pray."

"Ok," he nearly shrugs. This is our normal life. Both Matts had prayed for other people in the past who experienced healing.

"What are we praying for?" one of them asks.

"Taryn has really bad cramps."

Our kind believes strongly in the "laying on of hands" which in the case of illness typically means placing a hand on the infirm area of the body.

"Ohhh," says the second Matt, hesitation in his voice and eyes.

"I'll just touch your shoulder," says the first Matt.

Rachel places her hand on my abdomen. She says a short prayer out loud as the guys look on and pray softly. Business as usual.

Then, flutters.

Two distinct flutters.

Like the tips of a moth's wings inside my upper uterus in two separate locations followed by a soft bump against my lower uterus.

Exactly as if.

Something had fallen there.

I stand completely still. The trio is finished praying. They each look at me with concern.

"Guys, I felt something," I say. "Something *moved*."

"What?"

"Yeah. It was weird. Like butterflies inside."

"Praise God," one of the Matts says before they both disappear rather than hear any additional details.

Rachel's eyes widen with excitement.

"Seriously!" I assure her. "Something happened. I felt something fall."

"God is so good!" Rachel squeals.
We hug.
"I think I just got healed."
And indeed I did.

The next day,
and the day after,
and every day since,
I've had as much caffeine and tofu as I can stand.

ㅂ|

# My Ex-Future Baby Daddy

Initially, when I decided to move to Asia, I had China in mind. If not China, then Taiwan. I had been self-studying Mandarin Chinese for a couple of years, the first six months of which was spent just trying to hear the four tones of Mandarin before I could even say them back. That is a lot of struggle to toss aside without using!

During my Mandarin study, I started digging into pop culture and discovered Taiwanese American Wang Leehom[1]. His "Heroes of Earth" is the best Chinese fusion album you've *never* heard.

---

[1] The title single is "Heroes of Earth," (蓋世英雄). It's a mashup of traditional Chinese opera and hip-hop featuring BET Freestyle Friday's only Asian hall of famer and former Ruff Ryder, MC Jin.

During that season he was arguably the biggest Mando-pop star in the world. One of his singles featured an Asian girl in cornrows singing the hook and another Asian guy singing the chorus. It's a decent track serving up a lightweight flavor of R. Kelly and Jay-Z's, "Fiesta." The two guest singers were singing, not in Mandarin... but Korean?

When in doubt, check the comments. YouTube confirmed it:

> *"So good to hear wo ai ni and saranghae in one song!"*
> *"How come we don't see Rain in the video?!"*
> *"OMG Rain!!"*

I was intrigued. This "Rain" was a person! It's true we hear this man's breathy, buttery voice in the song and Leehom says his name in the video, but at no point is he seen.

My internet search began.

I found the music video for, "It's Raining," the lead single from Rain's (then) most recent album. The production value rivaled anything on MTV at the time.[2]

Rain enters an underground club flanked by personal security? An entourage? A door slams and suddenly, he's on stage. The music starts and Rain begins to dance. He is flanked by alternating successions of male and female dancers. His smooth

---

[2] "the time" being 2007. If you watch the "It's Raning" video, for context, this is the same year Flo Rida's #1 single had shawties all over the world getting low in Apple Bottom Jeans and "boots with the fur."

baby face peeks out from under his cap, eyes focused on the camera as his body undulates to the beat.

In the final third of the video he pulls a Michael Jackson power move, throwing his hand in the air with a shout. A burst of water splashes from the ceiling. The dancers continue unabated, their pleather-clad bodies glistening.

It was fascinating. It was somewhere between the spectrum of Bollywood and every Top 20 American pop song... somewhere I never knew existed.[3]

I listened to and watched everything I could find.

I downloaded bootlegs.

Rain's first... second... third and fourth cd.

The Japanese cd!

Music videos.

Concert clips.

I hated how much I loved it.

There's one song in particular called merely, "I" (나). It's a song about someone who can't stop loving someone else even though they know they should. I hate how I can't stop loving this song—the performance of this song.[4]

---

[3] And by "Bollywood," I'm very specifically referencing the dance scene that made Hrithik Roshan a star: *Ek Pal Ka Jeena* from *Kaho Naa... Pyaar Hai* (2000). Feel free to just start where the water drops from the ceiling of the night club at 4:04 in. Yes, you *can* see two of his three thumbs for most of the sequence but someone with such a perfect body has to have at least one flaw, right?

[4] Now that I hyped the song up, y'all prob gon' be extra underwhelmed but check out the video for 나 anyway! lol

Without fail, when Rain performs this ballad, he does a semi-striptease just before actual water falls from the ceiling and he body waves through the chorus.

He is serving up pale-skinned Usher with unbridled desperation and to this day, I can never quite drag my eyes from the scene of the crime.

After building his pop music career, Rain did some acting. The first Korean drama I ever watched was *Full House* (풀하우스). It's a fun adaptation of a Japanese manga featuring not only Rain, but two other incredibly handsome leading men, Kim Sungsoo, and my forever crush Daniel Henney[5].

The second Korean drama I ever watched was Rain's first, *Sang Doo, Let's Go to School* (상두야 학교가자).[6] Let me tell you what, I don't know who came up for the concept for this drama, or who approved it but, *Sir/Madam, I salute you!*

Someone managed to put a juvenile prison sentence, gigolos, a baby mama with an afro perm, child cancer, an old-fashioned love triangle, and the worst series ending of all time in one show. Y'all, Tyler Perry himself could not have come up with a more

---

[5] Also, at the time of print, Daniel's still single in these streets and I want him to know that I'm loyal. Look at that face. And the sweet doggie!

[6] Depending on where you live, *Sangdoo* is available on KBS or Kocowa or Viki or Amazon Prime. If you're picking just one, pick *this* one. I'm telling y'all!

needlessly complicated storyline.

I was here for all of it.

Rain led me to Korea.

I had never imagined I'd actually meet him.

*****

In May 2008, after having been beaten for the second year in a row for the *Time* 100 Reader's Poll by Rain, American TV personality Stephen Colbert invited Rain to his show for a dance off.

This consisted of Rain doing a few of his signature moves and Colbert giving 100% to some very comedic moves. The moment was just in time for the release of *Speed Racer*, an American film in which Rain plays a secondary character.

For his fans, myself included, it was thrilling to watch the two worlds collide.[7]

In the fall of 2008, Rain dropped his 5th album, "Rainism." The eponymous title track had a line about how Rain's "magic stick" would "make your body shake" which I found comically gratuitous. The Korean ratings board was *not* amused. The whole album got marked as explicit.

When tickets for the tour were released, I pinged my friend Hannah to go. We were both in Korea for

---

[7] Watch the Stephen Colbert clip. Skip the movie. Unless you really like video games and cartoons because that's basically what it is—all 2 hours and 15 minutes of it. *#justsaying*

just this sort of thing. We got decent seats and eagerly awaited the show.

I picked out my outfit in advance: a gold fabric mini-dress sheath. The back was open through the mid-torso with a small hand-tied bow and three opalescent buttons beneath. I love Korean fashion. If you're going to bare body parts, be cute about it, ya' know?

Hannah and I did what American girls do when they're on their way to see a favorite artist—we dressed like we were about to hit the club. When we got to the concert, I realized that this is not universal.

Not only were Hannah and I the only non-Asians in our section of the stadium—she with her naturally blond hair and me with my coffee brown skin—you could say we were flaunting our foreign assets.

The show was electrifying. Every bit as crass as expected...and more! I could not have anticipated Rain and his male dancers doing stripper pole work on stage. I didn't know whether I should close my eyes or my mouth after my jaw dropped. But the whole point of live performance is surprise, right?

I was surprised to see the family of four a few rows in front of us seemed to view the whole thing as wholesome entertainment. Mom, Dad, and elementary-school-aged children all bobbed their heads and clapped glow-sticks pleasantly to the beat.

*Why am I so easily scandalized?*

Rain sang, 너. It was every bit as salacious as

expected. As he was showered with water from above the stage, I believe I stopped breathing.

I am happy to report that I survived.

In the stadium, a few sections to the left of us were two Western-looking girls also dressed for a night out. Both were tall and thin.

One had on a bright red lipstick and a matching red wrap-around dress. With her stature, pale skin, and blond hair, she would probably stand out anywhere.

Our seats were in the risers of the stadium in a section that allowed us to see a staff-only hallway below us to the right. Various production team and facility staff could be seen milling about.

At some point, it became apparent a smartly dressed middle-aged man in a suit was watching us watch the show. Hannah pointed him out. When he saw me looking at him, he averted his eyes. Occasionally, I would check to see if he was still there. He didn't move for most of the show.

The concert ended around 10 p.m. Hannah and I exchanged notes on highlights of the show as we exited the stadium.

We talked about what we should do now that we were all hyped up and dolled up on a weekend evening. We waited for the crowd to clear before we headed to the subway.

"The night is still young," I said, because I like speaking in clichés. And because night life in Seoul truly doesn't start until midnight.

We exited through a side door of the stadium. In the distance, we saw two men smoking near a trashcan, illuminated by dim pathway lights.

"I think that's the guy from inside." Hannah noticed him first. "I just wanna see if that's him," she said, redirecting our path.

It was him.

Up close, we could see he was older than we assumed. Possibly late 40's. Maybe early 50's. Not very tall, still, very handsome.

"Hi," Hannah addressed him.

He looked startled.

"We saw you inside," she continued.

His companion was a 20-something dressed in American business casual. He looked on, trying to ascertain the moment.

"Hello," the man older stammered. "I don't speak English well."

"Oh...sorry," Hannah offered.

The young one put out his cigarette.

"Hey," he jumped in with perfectly accented English. "Where are you guys from?"

"We're American."

"Me too."

*That explains the clothing choice.*

"You guys like the show?"

We tell him we loved it and how we're both Rain super fans and...

The young guy sums up our conversation to the older guy in Korean.

"Wait, so you guys don't know who he is?"

Hannah and I both stare blankly.

"He's Rain's manager."

*Oh snap!* 대박!

One, or both, of us apologized for our lack of recognition. Our faces radiated both embarrassment and glee at our good fortune.

We all four exchanged names. The manager was "Jay" and the kyopo kid was "Danny."

"Are you guys busy later?" Danny asked. "You should come to the after party."

*Stay calm.*

*Answer cool.*

*Do.*

*Not.*

*Squeal.*

"We were just talking about what we're going to do next."

*Nice save, Hannah!*

"Where is it?" I ask casually, while my insides scream, *OH MY GOD!!!*

He explains that it's at a club somewhere between Apgujeong and Gangnam, aka, far from where we are and in much nicer digs.

Danny confirms with Jay in Korean then gives us the name of the club.

"Everyone will be there at midnight. You just have

to tell them that Jay said you can go in."

Ok. And ok.

"Yeah, we'll see you guys there in a bit."

Hannah and I take down Danny's number and walk off conscientiously containing ourselves until we were completely out of sight and earshot.

Squeals.

Giggles.

*Oh my god*s.

We had an hour and a half to grab a snack and powder our noses.

**\*\*\*\*\***

We had been warned the club wasn't easily accessible by public transportation so after grabbing lattes at a late-night café on the main drag in Gangnam, we caught a taxi to the club.

It was non-descript, fitting neatly in its surrounds. The only indicator was an unmarked, ornate set of double doors.

As we approached, I noticed three men in black suits and skinny ties in front of the door. They stood behind two tables that served as an additional barrier.

Another smartly dressed man was seated at the table holding several lists.

"Hi," I said to the man with the papers. "Jay said we could come in."

"Your name?" the man asked, slightly irritated,

flipping through the papers.

Neither Hannah nor I were on the printed list that had probably been made days prior to two hours ago. The man stated as much in both English and Korean.

"Jay told us we could come when we saw him at the concert."

"NO," he waved us away with an intensity I didn't care to challenge.

Two of the security were young, fit, and handsome. The third was large and in charge.

They didn't even acknowledge our presence.

I tried to make eye contact with the young handsome ones, utilize a little foreigner charm... no response. It was beyond disappointing and to be honest, out of the ordinary.

One of the aspects of being a highly visible foreigner in Korea is the amount of staring that occurs. Particularly when Hannah and I were together. We had taken to referring to the phenomenon as "Ebony and Ivory."[8] *#80sjoke*

Together, photos had been taken of us without our permission. Together, the prurient gaze of ajosshis was never far from us even under the most benign of circumstances. Together, we should at least be able to score acknowledgement and a smile from a couple of young security guards.

---

[8] Stevie Wonder and Paul McCartney made "Ebony and Ivory" such a lame song, it almost makes you think black folks and white folks should just go separate ways!

We were stumped. A call to Danny revealed only that everyone was "on their way."

Hannah and I moved away from the club entrance to sulk further down the sidewalk. I wasn't freezing but I definitely could have worn more clothes. We watched as an occasional person was permitted entry. We waited for what felt like an eternity.

Suddenly, we heard Danny's voice behind us.

"Hey," he said, mid-stride toward the gatekeepers of the club. He told them something in Korean. The man with the papers said something back. He wasn't having it. Danny said something else. He looked annoyed. I looked at Hannah. We both looked away from the scene.

Within a minute, Jay walks up. He is preoccupied with the people walking in beside him. Danny yells out to him, speaking quickly in Korean. Jay responds with about two syllables and the flick of his arm directed to the man at the table.

Danny heads to the door. The large security guard glares at Hannah and me as he opens the door. His gaze burns a hole in the back of my head.

\*\*\*\*\*

The club was the stuff of movies. The entryway belied the vast space inside. The room was a two-story high black box accented with drapes and chandelier light fixtures.

Music played but the dance floor was not yet occupied. A few young Koreans with drinks in hand bobbed their heads to the EDM tracks blaring through the speakers.

We followed Danny up a set of stairs to a table-service VIP area that overlooked the dance floor. A couple of men were already there. They greeted Danny and exchanged a few words.

One was a nattily dressed ajosshi in a clearly expensive tailored suit. The other was a member of the concert production staff. We exchanged introductions.

A couple of moments later, up the stairs sauntered the foreign girls we saw at the concert trailed by a few more Koreans. Red Dress, who had clearly been "pre-gaming" before she arrived, and her cute but sensible-looking Brown-Haired Friend.

I was relieved to see them. It would take some of the focus off of Hannah and me. At the moment, we were the only women and only visible foreigners.

The Brown-Haired Friend made eye contact and smiled. Red Dress was being chatted up by the Well-Dressed Ajosshi who was clearly old enough to be her, my, everyone's father. She gamely entertained him.

At some point staff moved us into an adjacent VIP room. It had black and near-black décor from floor to ceiling. The room was barely larger than the expansive half-circle booth and table in its center. There was (snug) seating for 10-12 people with a large flat screen TV on the wall opposite.

Well-Dressed Ajosshi directed us to have a seat.

Hannah and I slid into the booth. Brown-Haired Friend slipped in next to me.

Red Dress was at the end. The Ajosshi secured the spot closest to her. Danny took the other end of the booth closest to Hannah.

Another couple of ajosshis entered the room and talked with the first. They spoke with Red Dress. She chatted a bit in Korean.

Danny explained the well-dressed ajosshi was the manager of Rain's clothing line. The other two men worked for Rain's label.

They took in the four of us foreign girls with a curious glance.

I noted the room had no windows and neither did the door. Even private karaoke rooms have a frosted window pane. The lighting was quite dim. I wondered how many more men would appear.

A young kid from the nightclub staff brought a tray of food. He kept his head bowed and eyes low, placing the tray on the table and practically backing out of the room without a word.

I leaned over to Hannah, "If they put porn on that TV, I'm crawling out under the table." She laughed.

"I'm serious!"

"I might go with you."

We both laughed.

A man and a woman arrived to the room. The

woman left the door open behind them. They began chatting with the ajosshis. The food lightened the mood, offering another point of focus.

I introduced myself to Brown Hair. She was a Turkish girl studying Korean at Yonsei which is where she met Red Dress who was Russian. *Yes*, Red Dress had been drinking since earlier in the evening.

Of the two of them, Red Dress spoke the better Korean and it was her acquaintance who had gotten them free tickets to the show and the after-party invite. Brown-Haired Friend was just along for the ride.

After a bit, word came that we should leave this VIP room for a different room. This was conveyed through Danny and rough English on the part of several others.

This other room was already buzzing with activity. It was large enough for several dozen people to stand comfortably. The ceiling was about 10 feet high. One wall of the room was a series of ceiling-to-floor drapes.

The entire space was modern baroque: opalescent damask wallpaper, gilded velvet settees, a solid-wood center table set with trays of silver laden with fresh fruits, charcuterie, cheeses, and a continual flow of $200-a-bottle champagne. This was The VIP room.

The change of space was a relief but overwhelming. Hannah and I were serving up cuteness but these people were official glitterati.

We slid into the space behind Danny who entered the room seemingly unbothered.

As is my habit, I found a spot at the edge of the room with my back to the wall so I could take in the space. It appeared that everyone else knew several clusters of people. Perhaps it was just that they were all able to talk to one another and we weren't.

Danny suggested we should get drinks. I agreed. Having something to hold onto was a relief. After a moment, a youngish Korean guy recognized Danny and came over to greet him. Or us.

He was very interested in who Hannah and I were. He was handsome. Local, but with excellent English. He looked like a young Johnny Depp[9] but named Sunghoon. The interest was mutual.

Sunghoon was Rain's band director. Consequently, he seemed to know something about every person in the room. He pointed out the costume and makeup girls, music producers, and record label staff.

After a bit, he and Hannah settled into a comfortable banter. Danny excused himself for a phone call. I lingered a bit before noticing Brown Hair standing by herself. I approached her.

We both watched as Red Dress chatted up some of the record label staff while laughing gregariously.

"She really likes to have a good time," I said.

"Yeah." We both watched. "I don't know why she

---

[9] If you don't know what Johnny Depp looked like when he was younger, <u>look it up</u> now and thank me later.

keeps talking to that ajosshi," Brown Haired said, indicating Smartly-Dressed Ajosshi. "He kept touching our waists every time he passed by."

"Eww," I laughed nervously, making a mental note to avoid him.[10]

Behind Smartly-Dressed Ajosshi, a movement across the room by the mini bar caught my eye.

*That guy looks familiar. Is it—*

I lean into Brown Hair, "JYP is here!"

"Yeah. He's been here for a while."

*Oh snap.*

I slid over to Hannah, "Did you see JYP?"

"Sunghoon pointed him out when he came in."

*Clearly, I need better intel.*

I couldn't believe I was in the same room with one of Korea's biggest music producers and record label heads! Although he was the producer who made Rain a star, Rain had moved to his own label and was debuting his own groups.

Around this time of the concert, JYP was promoting his premiere girl group, The Wonder Girls, through a US tour and a made-for-TV movie all in

---

[10] I would like to take this moment to point out that Rain's fashion line, Six to Five, was *extremely* short lived—maybe two years? I'm sure it was this ajosshi's fault. There were rumors about misappropriation of funds and if you ask me, the kind of person who would snatch yo' waist is the same kind of person who would snatch yo' cash.

English.[11] He's not particularly handsome but he has a certain *je ne sais quoi* that is magnetic. I tried not to stare but I failed.

But it was ok. He was looking my way.

Really.

JYP leaned into a guy standing next to him. They looked at me while they spoke.

My surroundings faded as I focused in on him.

It was now or never.

I gripped my glass of champagne and walked over to JYP to introduce myself.

"Hi. I'm Taryn."

He looked surprised. Startled? He extended his hand.

"JY Park."

"Nice to meet you."

"Yeaaahh," he answered.

"I know who you are. Didn't you just get back from the US with The Wonder Girls?"

"Yeah," he looked surprised and pleased at this question. #*winning* "You kept up with the tour?"

"And the movie," I grinned. "I saw you guys were looking my way so I thought I'd come over and say 'hi.'"

JYP's sidekick laughed.

---

[11] The Wonder Girls' first single, "Nobody," was EVERYWHERE when it came out. To this day, you can run up on old K-pop heads and say, "I want nobody, nobody but you," with two claps and start a singalong. As for the TV movie, I have yet to meet anyone who's actually seen it. Speak up if you have!

"Ohhhh, I was looking for my *hoobaes* (후배)," JYP replied. "I heard there were some Yonsei girls here.[12]"

*Oh. Indeed.*

I bit my lower lip as I turned my head to follow his eyes. "They're over there," I said.

Red Dress and Brown Hair were chatting together at the other end of the room.

Where I belonged.

"I can get them for you," I offered, as my desire to escape proffered a pitiful excuse.

"Yeah. Tell them I want to meet them."

I was too filled with liquid courage to fully feel the humiliation of the moment as I marched over to the girls determined to fulfill his request.

"Hey," I interrupted them, "JYP wants to meet you guys."

The pair laughed in delight.

"Yeah, he told me to get you."

Red Dress grabbed Brown Hair's arm and pulled her along the length of the room to JYP.

---

[12] Y'all, this was a deep flex on JYP's part:

1) He pulled a humble brag about going to <u>Yonsei</u>, one of Korea's Ivy League Universities.

2) In this context, if I were a "Yonsei girl," the mention of the word, *hoobae*, would put me in a presence of mind to talk to him with more formality than I had just displayed. (후배 can be translated as "junior" in the sense of someone who is not as "senior" as you in whatever-it-is-you've-been-involved-in. This is used in school and work contexts often to remind everybody who's an O.G. and who's not.)

3) He let me know he was not looking at me without saying, "I was definitely <u>not</u> looking at you."

I observed their interaction. They were both tall, thin, and white with silky straight hair.

They radiated youth and the Korean image of "desirable foreign woman."

I retreated into my observationalist lens to lick my wounds. *Who is that next to JYP? I've totally seen his face before.*

I relocated Hannah and Sunghoon.

"Is that Mithra Jin?" I asked Sunghoon.

"Yeah. It's Mithra. Tablo is here too."

*Shunned by JYP and laughed at by Mithra Jin[13]. I'm wracking them up tonight!*

"Did you see the bathroom?" asks Hannah, her face lit with delight. "You should use it."

"Where is it?" *I could use a private space to recover from embarrassment right about now.*

She indicates a barely open door not far from the mini bar. *Of course that's where it is.*

"It's like, gold everything."

*Ooooooh. I do like me some interior design!*

"Hold my champagne."

I ventured to the restroom, doing my best to remain unnoticed by JYP and Mithra.

Fortunately, the VIP room was more crowded by this time so I was able to enter the lavish lavatory unobserved. It was delightful.

---

[13] Mithra Jin is one third of the rap group, Epik High. In 2009, they were one of the best known rap acts in Korea.

Have you ever been someplace where it took everything in you not to overstay your welcome? This little powder room was it. The ceilings were as high as the wider room adjacent with each wall clad in a deep black and gold jacquard wallpaper.

Gold light fixtures. Gold faucet hardware. Gold toilet paper holder. And a gold toilet bowl handle.

It was enthralling and disorienting.

*Should I sit on the toilet or do the public-toilet-hover?*

*Is this toilet actually public though?*

*It looks practically royal in here!*

*I think I'll enjoy it better if I sit—*

A knock on the door determines my decision.

"YES!" I shouted in acknowledgement and began hoovering.

I washed my hands in the beautiful sink, with the lovely hand soap, and braced myself to reenter a room that had gotten progressively louder.

When I opened the door, the Korean girl who was waiting looked surprised.

Then annoyed.

She brushed past me without acknowledgement.

I found my way back to Hannah. Sunghoon was off talking with a group of people.

"How was the bathroom?" she asked knowingly.

"Amazing!" I laughed. "He's really cute," I stated, indicating Sunghoon.

"I know, right," Hannah gushed. "He said his last girlfriend was a foreigner."

"Sounds promising," I replied, as we exchanged grins.

The room was abuzz with energy. I realized that several of the new editions to the room were Rain's backup dancers. I recognized a few of the men from Rain's music videos. A few of the women I recognized from the stage as they were still in full makeup.

They were all attractive and fit. They all also exuded a harsh, inhospitable energy. The women were literally the coldest chicks, I had ever seen in Korea and I was once shoved unprovoked by a 5'1" escort at a bar in Itaewon.

If a fight broke out with these dancers, Hannah and I were definitely losing.

Brown Hair found me. "They said Rain is on the dance floor, do you want to go down?" she asked, indicating the large window panes that were previously covered by ceiling-to-floor curtains.

We now had a second story view of the dance floor.

I went to the window to check for Rain. He was nowhere to be seen. Instead, I noticed another black girl with a white friend on the dance floor.

They were like an echo of Hannah and I but younger and casually dressed. The black girl waved at me in excitement. I waved back and gave her a thumbs up sign as I flashed a grin.

I turned back to the room to confirm to Hannah and Brown Hair that I didn't see Rain.

But I do see Rain.

In.

The.

Room.

RAIN. IS. IN. THE. ROOM!!!

All six-foot-one of him is less than 20 feet from me and I am so very frozen in fear of doing Really Dumb Things. *#rightfullyso*

He had showered and changed into a vest? Maybe a shirt? What mattered most was his unnecessarily-low-slung pair of distressed blue jeans and the fact that his top(s) were just short enough to leave a peek-a-boo panel.

This was the final date of the tour. His body was toned from months of daily dancing. He was close enough to his *Ninja Assassin* physique[14] for his body to hold a pelvic "V" yet sufficiently distant as to hold some softness. In other words: Perfect.

Rain blessed all of us with a full view. I wondered if he had gone commando to pull that off.

"Oh my god," Hannah, or I, or both of us squealed.

Rain greeted several people as he came in the room. He was accompanied by a young, pretty faced guy. It was one of the members of MBLAQ, a boy band that Rain had debuted on his label, J. Tune

---

[14] Google's got you for photo evidence on the *Ninja Assassin* physique. You're welcome.

Entertainment.[15] They opened for Rain during the tour.

There was a group of sophisticated young women sitting in the lounge chairs closest to the door. Rain spoke to them in an animated manner. They howled in laughter and met his energy in their verbal responses. I looked on in desperate curiosity.

He pushed the boy band member toward one of the women. The boy moved with hesitancy which caused increased laughter.

Another member of the band seemed to appear from nowhere. Rain grabbed him from the entryway and repeated the spectacle, depositing the second member with a different woman.

"Sunghoon, what are they doing?" Hannah asked.

"Rain is selling MBLAQ to those ladies."

"What?" I ask, not sure whether to laugh or panic.

"Like an auction?" asks Hannah. She's on the same frequency as me.

"Yeah. Like, 'Who wants to meet Seungho? Who wants to meet G.O.?'"

Definitely, a bit weird but everyone seemed to be having fun.

I slid over to the refreshment table to refill my champagne glass. When nervous, just drink more, right?

I stood near Hannah and Sunghoon as they chatted away. I took in the sight of everyone else in the room.

---

[15] MBLAQ's first single, "Oh yeah," was their biggest hit. *Oh well.*

I couldn't help but think, *How are we here?!* Simultaneously, one of the Korean girls seated nearby took it upon herself to pull rank.

Hannah was mid-sentence when the girl shouted, "Sunghoon-*ah!*" Then rattled off a question in Korean while glancing directly at both of us.

Sunghoon answered her, completely unaware of the subtextual mean-girling that was occurring.

Hannah turned to me eyebrows raised, "I might have to fight her!" she only half joked.

"I got your back 'cuz she's rude as hell," I laughed. Then I remembered the stone cold glances of the girl dancers in the other half of the room. As my buzzed brain calculated our chances I added, "I can't promise we'll win though."

We gave it a minute then Hannah pulled a power move: She placed her hand on the crook of Sunghoon's arm and asked him a question, her voice a bit too low in volume for the noise of the room.

Sunghoon immediately leaned in to hear what she was saying.

On Hannah's behalf, I served Interrupting Girl the stank eye.

By this time, Rain had come back in the room. He was followed by Tablo[16], Mithra Jin's bandmate.

---

[16] Tablo is the more famous member of Epik High. His academic pedigree garnered so much ire—he completed an undergrad and master's degree in English at Stanford University—"only to become a rapper," that a group of self-proclaimed online activists called,

They greeted JYP. My eyes followed Rain's every move.

Every greeting. Every bounce of his hair.

Of his jeans.

In my mind, or somewhere outside of it, I saw an image of Rain an arm's length from me. I lifted my hand—first finger, middle finger, and thumb outstretched—and slid my fingers into the little shadowed valley in Rain's jeans between his pelvis and his goodies. I closed my thumb and pulled him close.

In real life, my eyes grew wide with panic.

"You guys wanna meet Rain?" I heard Sunghoon say. "I can introduce you." *Did he even need to ask?!*

As soon as Sunghoon stepped away, I turned to Hannah. "Don't let me touch Rain, ok?"

"Ok," she laughed.

"No. I'm serious!" I grabbed her arm. "I <u>saw</u> myself touching him."

"Ok, girl!" Still perplexed, she assured me.

---

TaJinYo (타진요), harassed both Tablo and Stanford for over year claiming he had falsified his degree. Stanford ended up posting a statement to their website *in Korean* stating that Tablo was an alumni. Koreans <u>do not</u> play when it comes to education!

Bonus: If you're bored, you read how an admissions scandal at the best women's college in Korea led to the impeachment of the president of Korea. Look up, "<u>How Protests at a South Korean university led to the downfall of President Park Geun-hye.</u>"

If you're wondering about poor Tablo, he successfully sued the leaders of TaJinYo for libel. *#justiceserved*

Sunghoon took a few eternal minutes and then he was back.

With Rain at his side.

Arm's length from where I stood.

"My friends want to meet you," Sunghoon told him in English.

"Hello, nice to meet you," Rain greeted us with a light bow of his head. I watched his hair shift as he moved.

Time.
Stood.
Still.

"Hi," Hannah, or I, or both of us squeaked, followed, or not, by something equally uninspiring but fortunately not memorably embarrassing.

Sunghoon may or may not have told Rain that we were teachers.

And as quickly as he had appeared, Rain removed himself from Sunghoon's very successful attempt to gain clout with two very thankful foreign girls.

We were both beaming.

I was overjoyed! I had met Rain, the future baby daddy of my imagination. As much as I wanted to touch him, I didn't because I didn't want to get thrown out of the club.

*****

Little else was notable about our time in the VIP room. As we chatted the night away with Sunghoon, the room emptied. I watched Red Dress become progressively more drunk.

At some point Brown Hair accompanied her out of the room without returning. The Cold Faced Dancers and Interrupting Girl also left in their own time.

Eventually, only Sunghoon, Hannah and I were left in the room.

"We *have* to take pictures now!" I insisted. By this time, I had been holding back the urge for hours. Sunghoon offered to take pictures of me and Hannah.

I positioned myself on a black velvet and silver painted settee I had been eyeing all night.

I had not dared to sit while the real guests were still present. Now, I crossed my legs and grinned from ear to ear as I clutched my mini-purse.

This is the only evidence I would have of that night—two grainy iPhone 4 photos of myself with great hair and a brilliant smile.

So be it.

After our photo binge, we settled into a nearby table with a view of the dance floor.

The room below was much more full than before. In contrast, the VIP room was now completely still.

Suddenly, the door opened.

A thick-necked Korean guy walked in. He looked

surprised to see us there. He greeted Sunghoon in Korean as he scoured the refreshment table.

He tilted each of the champagne bottles until he found one that had not been opened. He snatched it off the table then came over and introduced himself.

"Hi. I'm Jin," he said in confident English. "Where are you guys from?"

Hannah and I introduced ourselves and stated our American nationality.

Sunghoon told us that Jin was the live video director for the tour.

"That's a really difficult job," I said in a tone of admiration, adding a question about the number of cameras used. Everyone likes to talk about their job. Even if it's just to complain.

Jin answered my questions in detail, lamenting the camera crew's inexperience. [17] My interest and curiosity won him over.

"... 우리말 할 줄 알아?"

My Korean language ability was next to nil at this point in my stay but I did pick up the word he used for Korean (우리말) and I knew enough to know the next predictable course of the conversation.

---

[17] Y'all, the camera crew was awful. They MUST have had to pull in some substitutes because I don't know how/why on earth you still don't know where to focus your camera after weeks and weeks of rehearsals! Rain doesn't ad lib very much but we were getting shots of empty stage, dancers' feet, and out-of-focus closeups 10-20% of the time. They literally could've called in the camera crew for my old church and they could've held it down better!

Sunghoon answered and Jin responded with a couple more sentences.

"I just came to look for champagne," Jin told us in English.

"Ok," Sunghoon replied.

Hannah and I sent Jin off with a courteous, "Nice to meet you."

"What did he say?" Hannah asked.

"He just wanted to know if you guys speak Korean. Rain and some guys are drinking in the other room. He said we could go there but everyone only speaks Korean."

What?

Why?

*Whyyyyyyyyyyyyyyyyyyyyyyyyyyyyyyyyyyyyy?*

At this point I had been in Korea for over year. If I had had any inkling this day would come, I would have devoted my every waking hour to study.

But alas, I. Had. Not.

When thy hour comes, be ye prepared.[18]

After this moment transpired, there was genuinely no reason to hang around any longer. Sunghoon and Hannah wanted to do another round of activities but I was done for the night. They headed out together and I walked out into the deserted 2 a.m. streets of Apgujeong in search of a taxi, musing over what could have been.

---

[18] Book of Taryn, Chapter 5, verse 1

# An Unfunny Addendum

*Before we jump into this chapter, I want to point out, as the title states, it's not fun. It's a quick reality check on racism/xenophobia (some), depression/suicide (a lot), substance abuse (yes), and women's safety (<u>always</u> watch your back).*

*If you're not in a good place mentally or emotionally, you can skip the chapter since I just summarized it for you in the previous sentence.[1]*

Whenever I tell stories about Korea, I see most people's eyes light up in wonderment at the unbridled excitement of newfound possibilities held by a far-off land. "You should definitely go," I inevitably

---

[1] A few resources if you need help:
- Global
  - Depression/Suicide - https://findahelpline.com
- Korea-only
  - Seoul Sisters - http://www.sisters.or.kr - 02) 338-5801
  - Emergency support for foreign women - 02) 1366

conclude, ending my monologue with a sunny smile.

I stand by this statement. It is one of the abiding undercurrents of this entire book—so much so that Korea should at least let me be in one of their tourism commercials. *Hint, hint.* No pressure.

Although the F-2-7 visa—for which I suffered through such illustrious vocabulary such as 얼굴 근육, the Korean word for "facial muscles,"[2]—yet still failed to attain, would be a far more precious gift but that is not the point.

I envisioned this addition to the book when I remembered the messages I received over the years through email, Facebook, or as comments on my YouTube vlogs. Most of my viewers seemed to be young women and few were well traveled.

One of the messages stands out because the writer was 1) a high school girl who 2) didn't seem to understand the first thing about living abroad as a foreigner. Like many young women, she had fallen in love with the glossy, perfected Korea of television dramas.

In this regard, she is not unlike all the folks outside of America who believe we are overrun with criminal activity—thank you *CSI* and *Law & Order*—and/or a

---

[2] For the nerds who care, this is not a particularly difficult bit of combined vocabulary but I remember it because I nearly cried through a test essay on facial expressions. It discussed whether or not animals were really making facial expressions or whether humans just imagined/perceived it. I understood that much but still failed the exam! ㅠㅠ

nation filled to the brim with gorgeous, vapid persons enjoying lives of leisure—thank you *every other show on television*.

But back to our young student writer. Our exchange went as follows[3]:

> hey...I'm planning to come to Korea...am african girl. how is the country? how they gonna treat me?? pls..thank u...

> Hi hon, Depends on what you're doing here and whether or not you speak Korean really. I have some African girlfriends who are students. They seem to be doing fine. For black girls, Korea's not the best place for dating tho. :/

> oh...r u saying it's impossible to have Korean boyfriend? also are they friendly? I don't want to spend my time with depression after going there...thank u again for ur answer to my question?

---

[3] For what it's worth, this was copied word for word from our exchange on Facebook.

No not impossible. Just keep your expectations realistic. Korea is very appearance oriented and a lot of people are still obsessed with white skin and light eyes and being skinny.

*Oh, the concerns of youth...*

I remember once reading on a message board a comment by a young woman who had never visited Korea. She waxed on about how much she was in love with the culture due to her obsession with K-pop and Korean TV dramas...so much so that she stated she was going to move to Korea and change her citizenship!

I hate to be the one to tell you this kids, but you can't just change your citizenship to wherever on earth you please—unless you're in possession of an excess $500,000+ USD or so...in which case I have a short real estate investment presentation I'd like to give you.

I'm not sure why but I find the idea of someone assuming that they would love a place they've never been enough to live there forever and forsake any chance of returning to their homeland kinda crazy.

Still, I was once a high school girl. I would've taken

the advice of any adult whose life I desired to live very seriously[4].

For that reason, this chapter is dedicated to you: the inexperienced traveler, the girls and boys with less than 25 years of life under your belts. Korea is a real place—no more or less wonderful than any other place on earth.

Often, when I'm with a group of black people and the subject of my having lived in Asia comes up, there is a pause in the conversation during which someone leans in a bit:

"What do they think about *us*?" they ask, because when it's just *us* we don't have to say who *us* is.

"They don't really," I reply.

Which is to say that we are generally not thought of until the moment we are seen.

American = White.

Expat = White.

Foreigner = White.

Because Chinese people are not "foreigners," they are Chinese. And Japanese people are just Japanese. Until they are "yellow monkeys," but by then things have gotten terribly out of hand.

If I had to sum up racism in Korea, I'd say it this way: *It won't get you killed.* That's far more than I can say for America, which to me means it's nothing to lose sleep about.

---

[4] Yes, *you*, Lisa Bonet. <u>Then</u>, <u>now</u>, and forever!

Sure a few taxis will avoid you and employers will toss your job application in the trash as soon as they see your cheery black face but heck, that could happen anywhere!

So what that one somewhat retarded kid on the subway glared at me for a full 10 minutes before throwing a wad of paper and snarling the equivalent "nigger" (깜둥이) as he exited the train: Could've happened walking down the sidewalk in Venice Beach instead! #truestory

Did I let the server at the neighborhood restaurant who snatched a seating pillow from beneath me as I sat on it get me—or my Korean Canadian friend who looked on in horror—down? No, I didn't!

*That moment of silence was dedicated to my LORD and Savior Jesus Christ for having my friend with me so that a middle-aged Korean woman didn't get cussed the ACT.TU.AL. HELL. OUT in two languages that evening. Amen?*

Sure, one of my Korean co-workers insisted that I must be good at *some* sport because #blackpeople. And a guy working at the Itaewon Taco Bell was dismayed that his greeting of "What's Up?" instead of "Can I take your order?" left *me* dismayed. Or the college kids who were super excited to fist bump me in greeting— *Thanks, Obama!*—as I stared at them in confusion.

These are the off-kilter things: the things that can make a bland day more interesting or a stressful day all the more unbearable. The things kids these days call "microaggressions." [5] Either way, they're just different versions of what it means to be a minority to a fascinated, yet poorly informed majority. (See: America.)

And that is what most of Korea's xenophobia-tinged racism is: the majority (Koreans) vs. Everyone Else. Southeast Asians draw one brand of ire; white men, particularly when dating Korean women, draw another. Africans receive one type of treatment, Eastern Europeans another.

There are small reminders in what you cannot do such as: easily receive a bankcard that will work overseas or use certain websites because you have a non-Korean Citizen Identification Number with which to register. This, in addition to a language barrier that renders most immigrants limited to elementary communication can take a toll on the psyche.

At one point, I had run into a bit of a visa problem.

---

[5] Y'all, I'm too old for the word "microaggressions." Either it was aggressive or not. That's like saying, "He 'mini-slapped' me." Just, *no.* I've experienced aggression, I've experienced ignorance, and I've experienced passive aggressive behavior. They all feel gross but they're each different and deserve different responses.

I had been a "resident tourist" for about nine months and needed to get a work visa for a university position I had been offered. I made an unwanted trip to the Mokdong Immigration Office in Seoul. This particular office has a reputation for shall we say, "staff burn out."

When my number was finally up, I approached the counter of a pessimistic-faced clerk. I want to believe she said, "How can I help you?" in Korean because that would've been polite.

Whatever it was she said, it caught me off guard because all of the clerks at the immigration office are able to speak English. In all the time I lived in Seoul, other than this occasion, the immigration officers always greeted me with, "Hello."

Fortunately, this was at the height of my Korean language ability, so I took the woman's cue and explained my situation in Korean:

*I'm on a tourist visa but I have a job offer. I need to change visas. Is it true that I have to leave the country to renew my visa?*

Her response was appropriately detailed.

I attempted to scribble a few notes down but in realizing that my ability to scribble Korean wasn't up to the task, I had lost track of the conversation.

Was she saying I need to go to *a Korean embassy... in America?!*

*No, I think you can go to any other country's Korean embassy*, I replied in Korean. My legal status, my job, my apartment—my entire life hinged on me getting this information right. I stopped for a moment and switched to English.

"Sorry. What am I supposed to do?" I asked.

"You should go back to your country," she said glaring directly into my eyes.

*Ok, so I did understand this heifer!*

I don't remember what I said after that but I do remember fire rising from my chest up to my ears as we stared at one another for what felt like an eternity.[6]

No matter where you are in the world, no matter who in the world you are, there is always going to be someone who doesn't want you there.

Don't make their problem your problem.

And to address *us* directly, "Have you been black all your life? If your answer is "yes," I think you can handle Korea.

❋ ❋ ❋ ❋ ❋

I've never been much of a drinker. (I vomited 15 minutes after my first drink of champagne but that's a story for a different memoir!) In Korea, I found myself drinking regularly. More than I ever have, or currently do. I have watched other expats descend into a respectable alcoholism—fulfilling work obligations while spending every recreational hour

---

[6] 화가 났어 y'all! Actual 火 in my eyes. If I was a <u>superhero</u>, she woulda died. ㅋㅋㅋ

with a can or bottle in palm, drifting from bar to
never-closing bar.

Perhaps it's depression that drives some to drink?
Living abroad is full of stressors beyond
communication difficulties. As missed birthdays,
births, weddings, even deaths, accumulate thousands
of miles and continents away, the sense of loss can
envelope you in a dark cloud that is difficult to escape.

I spent most of my first winter in Korea fighting
illness after illness while living in a drafty efficiency
apartment about the size of the average American
hotel room. I was also without heat in a city where the
high temperature for the day is often below freezing.

I went from my cold apartment, to the cold
outdoors, to our cold school. After my first semester
in Korea, I had descended into a darkness unlike any
I had ever experienced in all my years, despite
occasional bouts of depression.

I woke up, sometimes showered, dragged myself
to work, endured 12-hour workdays then dragged
myself home, usually stopping for crappy takeout on
the way: corn-topped pizza, Korean-style seaweed
rolls (김밥), or a bowl of egg ramyeon.

My descent was so precipitous that I hadn't
realized it had occurred—that I had gone from sad to
helpless.

At my lowest point, an unfriendly look from a
stranger would pierce my soul and send me into tears.
I cried on the subway, walking down the sidewalk, and

at home—alone and cold.

While I couldn't pinpoint what caused it, I knew that I was in a dangerous space emotionally. What I also didn't know at the time is that Korea has one of the highest suicide rates in the world, second only to Japan, and that's only in the years Japan doesn't slip up and let Korea have first place.

Any sociologist will tell you depression and suicide appear in clusters, and I had unknowingly landed smack dab in the middle of one.

Obviously, I didn't kill myself and I managed to find a way to feel fully human in Korea—Thank you L'abri Korea, The Philippines, and Jesus Christ. (I'll write about these in the next installment!)

Even now, when I think back on that first winter, I don't know how I managed to survive yet effectively sleepwalk through the last few weeks of 2008.

On the numerous occasions I've talked to fellow Americans about teaching in Korea at least one person will inevitably purr, "Oh! The students must be so polite," head tilted askew as they replay mental images accumulated from repeat viewings of *The King and I*[7] and that quiet Asian kid they sat next to in math class.

And to that I can only say, "Not really." That is not to in any way imply that the classrooms that I taught in resembled the '90s film *Dangerous Minds*. Not my

---

[7] "Getting to Know You," *is* a fabulously cute song but sorry, the experience is nothing like that.

classroom anyway.[8]

That said, for better or for worse, I witnessed two high school girls at my school being paddled by a teacher. On several occasions, I required rowdy students to stand in the back of the class with arms raised overhead as punishment for misbehaving.

In that regard, teachers do still have an air of authority long ago lost in America. I once used my best Korean to yell at a group of high school boys who were smoking on the edge of school property.

Word got back to the Korean staff and one of the older men joked that I shouldn't do such things and risk making the students angry. Considering the rate of pace at which Korea changes, I'm sure his words will come true. I doubt teachers in Korea will have the upper hand much longer.

Another issue in Korea that deeply concerns me is women's safety. "It's so safe in Korea," men say in a confident tone exuding absolute truth. "*So* safe," girls say, dragging out the *oh* sound a couple beats longer than necessary for emphasis.

Rather than respond as crassly as I could to make

---

[8] I do know a guy who had to deescalate a kid that pulled a box cutter on a classmate. And then there was another acquaintance who decided to let two boys fight it out even though one of them seemed as if he were going to hurl a chair at the other because he really couldn't pry apart feuding middle school students while recovering from a hernia!

Lastly, <u>Dangerous Minds</u>, spawned one of the most memorable '90s anthems ever. The movie was a'ight too.

my point, I will quote a line from *Jab We Met*, (one of the best Bollywood 'movies of all time![9]): "A girl traveling alone is like an open treasure box."

Thus sayeth the predator from every tribe and tongue.

Fortunately, unlike many places in the world, a non-drunk, single woman need not have much more fear for her safety than she would at a college frat party, which is to say that kidnapping is rare but all other sorts of assault and misdeed are not.

Then again, that depends on how you define kidnapping.

There are notoriously horrifying incidences of women being assaulted by taxi drivers in Korea and of women (generally when drunk) being put in taxis then "helped" by acquaintances or utter strangers into instances of sexual assault and even murder.

In a circle of six female friends, we have experienced:

- Masturbating taxi driver, 1
- Flashers, 3
- Masturbating stalkers, 2
- Stalkers with attempt to enter apartment, 2
- Date rape, 2
- Propositions for sex/prostitution by strangers, 2
- Groping on subway, 1

---

[9] *Jab We Met* is literally, my absolute-never-to-be-replaced Bollywood favorite. It's probably on Netflix. Watch it and thank me later, ok?

- Random drunk guys banging on apt door, 1

At the time I was leaving Korea in 2014, the government was just beginning to take sexual assault seriously as a *criminal* offense.

Sex crimes were generally considered a civil matter between the affected parties and their families—matters for which the perpetrator could *literally* buy the victim's silence and perps rarely ever darkened a jail cell. (The film *Silenced,*[10] which is based on a true story of sexually abused children, finally helped push the public to demand changes in the law.)

Old mindsets are difficult to break... including the idea that a blonde woman is most likely a prostitute. That was once true—in the days after the collapse of the Soviet Union scattered its most impoverished across Eurasia. Unfortunately, blonde hair is still a bullseye for salacious advances from the older generation of men.

Additionally, any experienced lecher knows that the vast majority of Western women in Korea live alone. "Do you live alone?" has become a running joke between certain friends and I because we were asked this so often during introductory conversations with Korean men.

---

[10] 도가니 aka *Silenced* (2011) tells the story of a public school teacher who discovers that students at a school for deaf children are being sexually abused by several of the staff. He pushes for justice against them but is thwarted by the police and other members of the community.

If you can't beat creepy perviness, might as well laugh at it!

Still, I would be remiss if I didn't leave you with a *Come-to-Jesus-Moment* that encapsulates all of the points I attempted to make above:

I was tagged in a semi-public Facebook post that was multiple paragraphs. The names of friends of friends of friends of the original poster littered the comments section.

He introduced the post by saying he was only using this method because the police had been uncooperative so if anyone knew anything that could help would they please let him know right away.

This guy's sister, a 20-something, was walking home alone in the foreigner area of Seoul (Itaewon). It was after hours—maybe 2 or 3 a.m.

Whether she was on the main strip of Itaewon or Haebangchon, I don't recall but I do know that she was obviously foreign and alone... "a treasure chest."

While walking, a white limousine pulled up beside her. A man jumped out and pulled her inside—inside, where three or four other men were waiting.

This girl screamed and fought—tooth, nail, foot, and fist. A few hundred feet later, they opened the door and pushed her out onto the sidewalk before speeding off.

Immediately, she called her brother. He called a Korean friend to translate. They took her to the local police department.

Frightened, scratched, and bruised, the girl gave her testimony. They explained about the limo. Surely, they could just search the license plate records and at least identify the owner of the car so they assumed.[11]

The police "filed" a report and weeks later, with no progress, the brother posted on Facebook. Both frightening and salacious, the story spread quickly among the American expat community.

"Have you ever seen a limo in Seoul?" we asked one another. "A white one?" No and no.

In the 5 ½ years I lived in Seoul, I saw a limousine only once.

About two years after the alleged incident, I was sitting with a friend at a noodle shop on the main drag in Itaewon. We were outside enjoying the weather.

I faced the street as I ate. I remember stuffing a bundle of noodles in my mouth then stopping cold.

Cruising past on the opposite side of the street was a white limousine. I bit through the wad of noodles and let the remnant fall back in the bowl.

My friend noticed the difference in my expression. As I began to explain, the limo passed out of sight.

Retelling of the tale dampened our mood tremendously as we each grimly considered ourselves fortunate not to be intimately acquainted with the details of what occurred that night.

Some people suggested the police were unwilling

---

[11] Because of the narrow, winding streets, limos are extremely uncommon in Korea. There are very few places to safely drive one.

to investigate because the perpetrators were wealthy, connected to organized crime, or perhaps both.

Despite prostitution being illegal in South Korea, Itaewon is the center of one of Seoul's most enduring, lucrative, and blatantly open sex trade districts. It is hard to imagine the police force in such a district taking an "unsuccessful" rape very seriously.

Naturally, that story is every bit as depressing as it is shocking. I hesitated to include it in this book but decided to because while they're not the worst law enforcement on the planet, the Itaewon police force deserves to be publicly shamed for their negligence in this matter.

Secondly, with every year that passes, I have less and less ability to resist the urge to become the aunty warning everyone to "have fun but not *too* much fun." *#sorrynotsorry*

That said, no experience worth having is completely easy or carefree. None of the negative experiences in this chapter took away from the beauty of my time living in Korea.

For every sketchy or annoying or mean person, there were at least two or three awesome or interesting or helpful people.

Otherwise, how on earth would I have survived as long as I did?

My first year in Seoul, I lived in a neighborhood called Banghwa (방화), in a suburb on the edge of the city border. Judging by the reactions of several of the senior citizens in the neighborhood, there weren't very many foreign faces in the area at the time.

This was the year during which I survived on "crappy takeout" which included frequent visits to a little chain called Pizza School.

The place is called Pizza *School* for a reason. The clientele is mostly middle and high students sharing an affordable afterschool snack with friends...and foreign teachers looking for something familiar.

I went there at least once a week because the menu had English <u>and</u> pictures, and the shop was right outside one of the subway exits on the main street, right across from my apartment.

I always ordered a "combination pizza" which is pretty much a "supreme" in America: tomato sauce, mozzarella, pepperoni, sausage, green peppers...plus corn. Yes, the stuff that grows on a cob.

I only made that mistake once!

On my next order, this being the olden days before smartphones, I used the picture menu to explain that I didn't want any more of that yellow stuff on my pizza.

The ajumma who ran the store spoke no English but she had a pleasant, bright demeanor. She understood. And never forgot!

Every time after that, when I'd enter the store, she'd greet me warmly in Korean, ask if I wanted the combination pizza, without corn (yes, please!), and ring it up straight away.

She'd say little things to me in Korean and I'm sure she could tell by my answers—or lack thereof—that I couldn't really understand. Still, I appreciated her treating me like "a regular person."

A few months into this pattern, I popped in for my usual order. By this time, I was beginning to understand a little Korean.

"Your friend stopped by earlier," Pizza Ajumma told me in Korean.

"제 친구요?"[12] I clarified.

"Yes. She always orders the bulgogi pizza," she responded with a smile.

I laughed a little, not sure if I had understood correctly, then thanked her in Korean as she handed me my pizza.

Outside the restaurant door, I grabbed my phone, slid it open and called Izzy.

"Hey, did you go to Pizza School earlier?"

"Yeah, I did," she laughed. "Why?"

"The ajumma told me 'my friend' came in there. She said you got bulgogi pizza."

"She always remembers everyone's order!" Izzy exclaimed.

"I'm surprised she can tell us all apart," I said. "I almost thought she meant Candace in my building, not you."

---

[12] "My friend?"

"No. She remembers everybody," Izzy said. "The white people too."

We both laughed.

It's the little things, the little places, ordinary people, that make the difficult bearable. When I think of Banghwa, I sometimes think of my cold apartment but I *always* think of Pizza Ajumma.

I wonder if her shop is still there and whether or not she's memorizing the faces of a new set of young foreign teachers stopping by for an ok pizza and a friendly greeting on their way home from work.

I certainly hope so.

타미

# Thug Life

He's from your hometown," my friend told me, as if this were a statement of quality assurance.

My hometown is best known for having a two-part name—Newport—the easily acceptable part, and "News," the second part, marred with all the errors of poor naming choices and improper marketing conventions. It also has the effect of making people confused about what you've just said.

Call Center Clerk:  Ok, your state is Virginia...
                    What's the city name?
Me:                 Newport News.
Clerk:              Newpor– Sorry?
Me:                 New. Port. News.
                    Like a newspaper.
Clerk:              (Laughs nervously.)
                    Oh, ok. Sorry.

Sorry is right. The only thing[1] that puts Newport News on the map is Michael Vick, the NFL quarterback convicted of owning a pit bull fighting ring. It was appropriately titled "Bad Newz Kennels."

People probably took the name as a sign of malice on his part but "New Bad Newz" genuinely is the town nickname among the 30-and-under set. No ill-will intended. It's just a reference to pistol whippings and murders on the evening news.

So this guy my friend was trying to set me up with was from my hometown. Great. Perpetually single, I shouldn't have been so smug. I should have been glad someone was trying to hook me up with anyone at all.

Asia is not the best place in the world for a non-Asian girl to find a date.

Do an internet search for "Western girls dating Asian guys" and half the search results are about how Western guys can date Asian girls.

Because that's what actually happens.

Asian girls are quick to date Western guys but Asian guys are not so quick to leave behind the perks of millennia-old patriarchal culture. Guys come to Asia and partake of the buffet of available girls; girls come to Asia and eat the scraps off the dating dining table.

---

[1] To be fair, the legendary jazz singer Ella Fitzgerald was born in Newport News but I didn't know that until after I wrote this and she was only *born* there. I concede her greatness to New York City where she grew up.

Which is all to say, that my friend is a good friend for trying to set me up—essentially offering me table food—even if her choice of entrees was potentially questionable.

"He said he used to own a hip-hop clothing store," she continued. I envisioned a stockroom full of early 2000s hip-hop attire:

*Oversized basketball jerseys that fall to the wearer's knees.*

*Shorts that are so long, they rival pirate pants, but so wide, one 7-year-old child could fit in each leg.*

*Endless rows of pullover hoodies.*

My mind was lost in the imagery of clothing weighed by superfluous fabric.

"I told him about you. He wants to meet you."

"Really?"

"You guys are about the same age. And he had a black girlfriend before."

"He's a real Korean?"

This truly is the crux of the issue.

"Yeah. He just moved to the US for college and he stayed."

There are several things you must know to understand the significance of these statements: 1) Real Korean guys don't date black girls. 2) I don't date "interracial virgins."

While these statements are absolute, the essence of each is as true as can be. Statistics can prove the first fact and my experiences have cemented the second.

If, at our time of meeting, you have not checked "one or more boxes" on your racial dating resume, I don't care to be a part of your dating reeducation primer.

*We're looking for someone with two to four years' experience. Sorry.*

"So why is he back in Korea?"

"He got deported."

"Oh my God! Are you *serious*?!"

"Yeah but it's nothing bad. His visa ran out. He's not like, a criminal."

I wish I could send the expression on my face through the phone: *Incredulity* + *"Not Amused."*

"But he goes to church! I know you like that stuff."

Honestly, after spending my 20's with detailed lists of requirements for my potential dates, the Big 3-0 narrowed my dating wish list down to three things: the guy's gotta be smart, Christian, and good (enough) looking.

"I'm gonna tell him to call you, ok?"

Notice the words, "no criminal record" are not on that list.

"I hope I don't regret this, but ok."

After all, I *am* from Newport News.


This guy and I started off 21st century Korean style: text messaging through the KakaoTalk app. It's much better than regular phone texting because there's a wide selection of animated emoticons and people always post photos of themselves in their profiles.

This guy, Tommy, as he listed himself, was just my Korean type: small eyes that folded into little half-moons when he smiled, high cheekbones, and medium-full lips. Good (enough) looking? *Check!*

In his photo he also wore black thick-rimmed glasses that gave the trendy impression of intelligence. Definitely a good sign.

After a couple of days, we progressed to a phone conversation which, in true East Asian style, centered around work schedules. He was working in Paju, a small town closer to North Korea than downtown Seoul. I lived in downtown Seoul, nearly an hour from Paju.

I worked in the afternoon. He worked all day, 6 or more days a week. (On this continent, there is no mercy for a man who neglects Work, his eternal mistress.)

I enjoyed listening to his voice on the phone—*check plus!*—but rather than pursue, I resigned myself to letting this ill-fated arrangement fall to the wayside.

Then, I got a phone call.

"Hey, what are you doing tomorrow?"

It was Tommy.

"Same as usual. Class, then I'm free after 1."

"Ok. Let's have lunch. Can you meet at 1:30?"

"Ok."

"Do you have a business card?"

"Uh, yeah..."

"Make sure you bring your business card."

*I should probably be telling <u>him</u> that. Who knows what this guy is about? There better be some kind of business sweepstakes involved.*

"I'll pick you up at your school."


So there I was the next day on the sidewalk near school peering into the windows of cars trying to distinguish a particular Korean I'd never met from all the other Koreans I'd never met who were driving by. He drove a small late-model SUV. Definitely not a city boy. Seoul boys prefer sleek sedans. Still, I appreciated the curbside service. "Car dates" of any kind are hard to come by in the city.

"Hey! Nice to meet you. You look good!" he exclaimed as I hopped into the car.

"Hi," I squeaked out nervously. *I think I just got "hollered at."* My mind was trying to absorb the sensory incongruity of a Southern hip-hop influenced lilt flowing from a Korean face in the middle of Seoul.

"Your girl told me you from *Newpert News*." He pronounced each word as if we were standing on the edge of the Chesapeake Bay.

"Yeah. You used to live down there, right?"

"Yeah. All my homeboy's still living down there. You know where 34$^{rd}$ street is?"

*Ah, but his grammar is still Korean.*

*Did he just say "four-d?" Oh wait, I didn't answer yet...*

"Kind of." It's downtown and I'm from midtown.

"That's where my shop was."

*Yup. Ok.*

"You speak real good."

*Sound effect: record scratching.*

"I'm a teacher," I reply without much thought because my brain hurts. Tommy's statement had so much subtext it could fill a critical theory essay. Tommy misses all of it and continues.

"My homeboys, they talk real different..." On the last word he slows, not sure how, or whether to continue. I realize my eyebrows are raised as far as they can possibly go without burrowing into my hairline.

"I teach English so I have to use standard pronunciation and grammar," I say in an attempt to smooth things over.

"Do you have your business card?"

"Sorry!" I had forgotten it.

"For real? I'm gonna get in trouble with my boss 'cuz I said I gotta appointment in Seoul today. It's real serious 'cuz I been having some troubles at work."

*We've just met and I'm already ruining his life.*

"I forgot them at home but I don't live that far from here. Maybe 15 minutes. You can drop me off after we eat and I'll get it for you." This seemed an agreeable solution.

"Do you know any good places around here? 'Cuz I don't want to eat Korean food."

I was glad he said it first so I didn't have to. I suggested a little shopping mall between school and my apartment with a Pizza Hut.

As we drove near the entrance of the mall, Tommy noticed several black guys wearing polo shirts with upturned collars.

"See, that's the nice one right there." He looked at me for confirmation. Unfortunately, I am woefully unaware of men's casual wear clothing trends.

"That polo, right...the pink one with the white on the collar is a Tommy Hilfiger, the real one. I wish I was wearing that right now. Instead of this."

"This" was a clean white button down and flat front British tan khakis. And a khaki double-breasted trench coat. He looked *delicious*. Oversized polo shirts be damned.

We continued for a moment in silence and I finally heard the radio. It was Notorious B.I.G. The song ended and was followed by Tupac Shakur. Which was when I realized we were not listening to the radio after all.

"Is this Biggie and Tupac?"[2] I asked as we pulled into the parking garage. I hoped this musical selection wasn't chosen for my benefit.

"Yeah. I love Tupac," Tommy answered while backing his SUV into the spot like a *gangsta*. Using a single hand that barely grasped the steering wheel, he leaned back as he turned it, gliding the car into a parking space.

I watched this display of bravado and giggled to myself as I imagined Tommy's pale porcelain lower abdomen with the words "THUG LIFE" arched across in homage to Tupac's iconic tattoo.

Lunch was interesting. Unlike Tommy, *I* was aware that he garnered a bit of positive attention because of his height and impeccable dress. The two of us together were also a bit of a spectacle for an area of town popular with the homeless population.

Perhaps Tommy was overly nervous. He found the restaurant menu choices confusing even after the waitress explained them to him Korean. I explained the ordering system again in English. He told me to make the final decision on the order.

He complained about being back in Korea, listing all the foods he missed from America. He asked about

---

[2] If you are somehow unawares, they are both chart-topping '90s rappers who, due to a wildly publicized East Coast/West Coast feud, suffered early deaths due to gun shootings.

my life. I told him about studying Korean, and teaching English, and salsa dance lessons, and producing indie films just for fun. To this he said, "You really busy, huh?" and I recall nothing that was said in the restaurant afterwards.

He graciously paid for lunch and we left with a slim margin of time for a stop by my place.


We chatted a little as we drove along.

"Why you studyin' Korean?" His voice leaked a hint of accusation. "You don't need to. You already speak English."

I laughed at this. It's true. In the city of Seoul, one need not speak Korean.

"You wanna marry a Korean guy and stay here forever?"

"I could. I don't mind."

*Cue: Stoplight.*

*Cue: Pregnant woman in third trimester on crosswalk amidst crowd of pedestrians.*

"You wanna be like her?"

"Pregnant?" *This has got to be the worst-executed offer for sex ever!*

"You said you wanna get married. You wanna have babies?"

"Maybe? I'm not sure yet."

Tommy turned to me.

"Everybody wanna have kids."

*Just drive the car,* I say with my eyes.

"I'm kind of scared of being pregnant. I definitely wanna get married though."

"You really like it here?"

"Yeah. It's no worse than anywhere else." *Anywhere else* featuring Newport News predominately.[3]

"Man, I never wanted to come back to Korea. Did your friend tell you I got deported? I can't go back to US for seven years."

She's a good friend. Of course she mentioned it.

"Why do you like this place? I don't like Koreans."

*What is this? The confessional booth on MTV's The Real World?!*

Since that seems to be the case, let me take a moment to address our unmarried gentlemen readers separately:

First, let me confirm some rumors: If a woman is really into you, *yes* she has imagined what your collective babies will look like. (Tommy and I would have produced world-class models.)

If she is interested in marriage, she's measuring what kind of *father* you'll be and whether she can stand adding/hyphenating your name next to hers. I'd

---

[3] Rebuttal via the <u>Newport News Tourism Board</u>'s description of the city: "Newport News' great location and rich history, which begins shortly after the founding of Jamestown, has shaped the city into what it is today. Located on the banks of the Hampton Roads harbor in southeastern Virginia, Newport News is located near Hampton, minutes from Williamsburg and a short drive to Virginia Beach and the Atlantic Ocean." *#wegotwater*

decided long ago, I'm ok with being a Kim or Choi.

Unfortunately, our hero Tommy had just undermined his fathering potential by revealing that he found no use in his mother tongue, hates his homeland, and has beef with his people.

Kids raised by parents with similar views usually write motherland journey memoirs about alienation and spending lots of time in therapy after years of drug abuse and levels of promiscuity frowned upon by the Centers for Disease Control and Prevention.

Secondly, gentlemen, have no doubt, you're being weighed in the balances. Don't be found wanting.

I may not be excited about the idea of pregnancy, but I would like to feel confident that if I end up on the Mommy Track, I can trust my husband not to scar our progeny by alienating them from their fragile biracial, dual-citizenry identities.

Tommy and I ended our date with the business card exchange and promises to stay in touch. I sent the occasional text message. He called a few times but we never met again.

Several weeks later, my friend, checked in.

"I was chatting with Tommy online. He said you never message him."

*Oh my God. Did this grown man* _tattle_ *on me?!*

"I told you about our date. What the heck are we going to talk about? It's awkward."

"Well, he seemed nice. You didn't really give him a chance."

"I *did* give him a chance. I went out with him."

She didn't reply. The scorn of silence is better to give than to receive.


Nearly a year to the day of our first text message, Tommy messaged again. It had been several months since we were last in contact. I noticed his profile picture had changed. The photo was of him and a woman. They were smiling, heads nestled closely together in a way that screamed, "COUPLED." She looked so much older than him, she could have been his aunt.

"Who's in your picture?" I texted back.

"My fiancée."

"Oh wow. Congrats?"

*No, erase the question mark. That's rude.*

"Congrats!"

"Thank you...she is Japanese."

Real Korean guys don't marry Japanese girls.

She must be a Tupac fan.

안녕히 계세요!

# The Outro

Thanks for taking this journey with me. Assuming you didn't just skip to the outro without reading the entire book, you've suffered through a great deal of rambling. *I heart you!*

I used Seoul in the title of the book and while I described a lot of happenings there, I don't feel like I gave the city itself enough time to shine. Forgive me a few gratuitous paragraphs I'll call, *"Baring My Seoul."*

*Seoul has its own river, the Han. There are pockets of greenspace all along the river and breathtaking night views from its 31 bridges. In the middle of the Han River are several islands. There's a movie about a man getting stranded on one of the smallest islands[1] but the biggest, Yeoido, is also home to one of the world's largest churches and my favorite greenspace, Yeoido park.*

*Seoul also has its own mountain, Namsan. If hiking is your thing, Koreans are your kinfolk! I had never experienced people taking on a leisure activity with such scheduled intensity before living in Korea.*

*Suffice it to say, any given weekend at 10 a.m., while you're heading up a mountain trail, there are crews of senior citizens dressed in full hiking sets (sometimes matching!) who are heading back down to grab an early lunch.*

*Seoul is Christian. At least visually. Red neon crosses dot the hilly landscape as churches mark the night sky from hilltops between skyscrapers.*

*Nearly every neighborhood has its own flavor. There's traditional tea houses, traditional Korean homes ( 한옥), and a historical palace in Anguk.*

*There's upscale restaurants, clubs, and lounges in Gangnam. And like everywhere else in the world, the immigrant ghetto in the middle of town (Itaewon) is already steeped in gentrification.*

Again, I love Seoul. I spent some of the best times of my life there. It was both liberating and exasperating all at once!

If you take nothing else away from this book, it

---

[1] (김씨 표류기, 2009) *Castaway on the Moon.* Ultimately, it's a comedy about a man who unsuccessfully attempts suicide and finds love in the process. What's not to like?

should be that in Seoul you can find all sorts of people and all sorts of opportunities.

Seoul is every bit as much as beast as—though a different breed than—New York City and every bit as polarizing. Seoul is fierce and fascinating and even funny, but metropolitan life devours the unprepared.

I certainly didn't know what hit me.

Still, for all the good (and bad), I owe Seoul a great debt. It is in Seoul that I began to feel American—that I first began to understand the weight of the quasi-colonizer into which I was born.

The ubiquity of my mother tongue both—"standard English" and the cool way black folks talk when we're chillin'—the visible presence of Christianity and Korean reinterpretation of hip hop all swirled together in a delicious disorientation that placed me both in the center of every moment and somehow on the sidelines of ever truly being able to comprehend it.

So this, *Bearing My Seoul*, is my best shot. It's my life, my second city, and my soul laid out as truthfully as if I'd told it to you face-to-face.

I hope you enjoyed it. Better yet, I hope it made your view of the world a little bit bigger and your curiosity a little bit broader.

May we meet some day on the way to a new adventure!

# About the Author

TARYN BLAKE holds a BS Journalism Degree ☺ and a Masters in English and Creative Writing. She uses neither of these in her day job managing software.

*Bearing My Seoul* is her first book. She hopes everyone will buy multiple copies of it so that writing can be her day job instead.

# Keep in touch.

**Seriously, thanks for buying the book! If you've enjoyed it, please leave a review wherever you bought your copy.** Reviews really help like-minded readers discover the book!

If you're bored and want to see the original Bearing My Seoul videos on YouTube, you can find them at youtube.com/user/BearingMySeoul.

Leave a comment or two and let me know what you think. If you use the hashtag, *#bearingmyseoulEXP*, I'll know that you've come from reading the book.

**Also, I'm cooking up retellings of a few other true stories you might be interested in.**

If you'd like to keep in touch with my future projects, head over to my publishing website.

Until later, friends!

Sign up for the mailing list at Gold Apple Books.com

# Keep up with a busy life.

It's a lot simpler if you plan for it. I do this with pen and paper every single day and have for several years now.

**I created a series of daily planners.**

I tried so many planners trying to find one that combined my favorite elements of Korean planners—habit trackers and hour-by-hour schedules—with space for affirmations, gratitudes, and daily wins.

There wasn't an option, so I made one.
Actually, several!

**TODAY IS THE DAY.**
**Available in dated and undated editions.**

Buy at *goldapplebooks.com*  Gold Apple Books